LEARN TO
Knit Socks

Treat for Your Feet, page 34

www.companyscoming.com
visit our website

Ribbed Anklets, page 31

Learn to Knit Socks

Copyright © Company's Coming Publishing Limited

All rights reserved worldwide. No part of this book may be reproduced, stored in a retrieval system or transmitted in any form by any means without permission in advance from the publisher.

In the case of photocopying or other reprographic copying, a license may be purchased from the Canadian Copyright Licensing Agency (Access Copyright). Visit www.accesscopyright.ca or call 1-800-893-5777. In the United States, please contact the Copyright Clearance Centre, www.copyright.com or call 978-646-8600.

Brief portions of this book may be reproduced for review purposes, provided credit is given to the source. Reviewers are invited to contact the publisher for additional information.

The contents of this publication were provided especially for Company's Coming Publishing Limited under an exclusive license agreement with the copyright owner, DRG Texas, LP ("DRG"). The contents are not available for commercial use or sale outside of this publication but are intended only for personal use. Every effort has been made to ensure that the instructions in this publication are complete and accurate; however neither DRG nor Company's Coming Publishing Limited can be held responsible for any human error, typographical mistake or variation in the results achieved by the user.

First Printing April 2010

Library and Archives Canada Cataloguing in Publication
Learn to knit socks.
(Workshop series)
Includes index.
ISBN 978-1-897477-35-9
1. Knitting. 2. Knitting--Patterns. 3. Socks.
I. Title: Knit socks. II. Series: Workshop series (Edmonton, Alta.)
TT825.L42 2010   746.43'2   C2009-904371-8

Published by
Company's Coming Publishing Limited
2311-96 Street
Edmonton, Alberta, Canada T6N 1G3
Tel: 780-450-6223 Fax: 780-450-1857
www.companyscoming.com

Company's Coming is a registered trademark owned by Company's Coming Publishing Limited

Printed in China

The Company's Coming Story

Jean Paré grew up with an understanding that family, friends and home cooking are the key ingredients for a good life. A mother of four, Jean worked as a professional caterer for 18 years, operating out of her home kitchen. During that time, she came to appreciate quick and easy recipes that call for everyday ingredients. In answer to mounting requests for her recipes, Company's Coming cookbooks were born, and Jean moved on to a new chapter in her career.

In the beginning, Jean worked from a spare bedroom in her home, located in the small prairie town of Vermilion, Alberta, Canada. The first Company's Coming cookbook, *150 Delicious Squares*, was an immediate bestseller. Today, with well over 150 titles in print, Company's Coming has earned the distinction of publishing Canada's most popular cookbooks. The company continues to gain new supporters by adhering to Jean's "Golden Rule of Cooking"—Never share a recipe you wouldn't use yourself. It's an approach that has worked—millions of times over!

Company's Coming cookbooks are distributed throughout Canada, the United States, Australia and other international English-language markets. French and Spanish language editions have also been published. Sales to date have surpassed 25 million copies with no end in sight. Familiar and trusted in home kitchens around the world, Company's Coming cookbooks are highly regarded both as kitchen workbooks and as family heirlooms.

Company's Coming founder Jean Paré

Just as Company's Coming continues to promote the tradition of home cooking, the same is now true with crafting. Like good cooking, great craft results depend upon easy-to-follow instructions, readily available materials and enticing photographs of the finished products. Also like cooking, crafting is meant to be enjoyed in the home or cottage. Company's Coming Crafts, then, is a natural extension from the kitchen into the family room or den.

Because Company's Coming operates a test kitchen and not a craft shop, we've partnered with a major North American craft content publisher to assemble a variety of craft compilations exclusively for us. Our editors have been involved every step of the way. You can see the excellent results for yourself in the book you're holding.

Company's Coming Crafts are for everyone—whether you're a beginner or a seasoned pro. What better gift could you offer than something you've made yourself? In these hectic days, people still enjoy crafting parties; they bring family and friends together in the same way a good meal does. Company's Coming is proud to support crafters with this new creative book series.

We hope you enjoy these easy-to-follow, informative and colourful books, and that they inspire your creativity. So, don't delay—get crafty!

TABLE OF CONTENTS

Foreword 7 • Knitting Basics 8 • Sock Basics 16

Socks for Women

Keep her feet in style with this assortment of designs, colours and patterns.

Fancy Lace Socks,
page 42

Simple Self-Striping Socks, page 45

Man's Racing Stripe
Socks, page 74

Socks for Men

Keep his toes warm with socks made for rugged use and for relaxing at home.

Fancy Fair Isle Socks, page 68

TABLE OF CONTENTS

Socks for Children & Teens

Treat their feet with socks in fun colours and patterns for everyday use.

Socks for Babies

Baby's toes will stay toasty warm and looking cute as ever in these socks.

Little Tike Toe-Up Socks, page 108

Wee Baby Bamboozle Socks, page 112

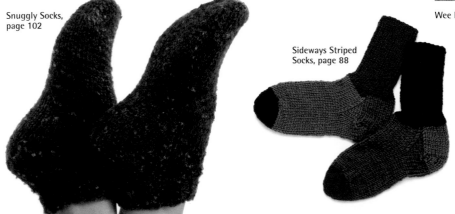

Snuggly Socks, page 102

Sideways Striped Socks, page 88

Make it yourself!

COMPANY'S COMING
CRAFT WORKSHOP BOOKS

LEARN TO *Sew for the Table*

48 easy-to-make projects
Step-by-step instructions
Colour photos of every project

LEARN TO *Knit for Baby*

Kids LEARN TO *Knit, Quilt & Crochet*

27 easy-to-make projects
Step-by-step instructions
Colour photos of every project

LEARN TO *Quilt With Panels*

LEARN TO *Knit in the Round*

LEARN TO *Make Cards With Photos*

LEARN TO *Craft With Paper*

LEARN TO *Bead Jewellery*

89 easy-to-make projects
Step-by-step instructions
Colour photos of every project

CRAFT WORKSHOP SERIES

Get a craft class in a book! General instructions teach basic skills or how to apply them in a new way. Easy-to-follow steps, diagrams and photos make projects simple.

Whether paper crafting, knitting, crocheting, beading, sewing or quilting—find beautiful, fun designs you can make yourself.

For a complete listing of Company's Coming cookbooks and craft books, check out
www.companyscoming.com

FOREWORD

Socks are a never-ending source of pleasure for knitters. Since they can easily be packed in a tote to take along, socks are great companions to work on while you're out and about—so even while on the go, you can knit socks for yourself or pairs to give away to family and friends. Who wouldn't love some stylish, hand-knit socks to keep their feet warm on the coldest days?

To help you learn to knit socks, this book begins with two great how-to sections. These are invaluable resources that will help you understand each technique from start to finish. Step-by-step instructions along with illustrations will help you with casting on, working in the round, doing short row toes and heels and successfully finishing the sock. Techniques for both Toe-Up and Top-Down socks are included.

People have been knitting socks using double-pointed needles for many years, but circular needles have recently become popular as well. One method uses two circular needles to work in the round, and the Magic Loop method uses just one circular needle. No matter which method you decide to use, clear directions will help make your sock-knitting experience successful and enjoyable.

Creative patterns and a variety of designs are given for making women's socks. We've included styles ranging from anklets to knee-highs. There are socks for everyday wear, socks in a variety of stitch patterns and colours and even socks to wear with flip-flops.

For the man in your life, try knitting some boot socks— they make a great substitute for slippers to wear around the house. Use self-striping yarns to make creating striped socks a breeze.

Teens, children and babies are not to be left out! For your next baby gift, try knitting a cute pair of booties. Stitch vibrant socks for both boys and girls using self-striping or bright-coloured yarns. Even your crazy teens will fall in love with a warm pair of hand-knit socks made just for them.

It's time to get started! Full-page colour photos and clear, step-by-step instructions with illustrations make it easy. Enjoy each stitch as you learn to knit socks for the whole family!

Kids' Boot Socks, page 91

KNITTING BASICS

Knitting With Beads

Threading beads onto yarn is the most common way to knit with beads.

1. Before beginning to knit, thread half of the beads onto your skein of yarn using a bead threader. (These will be used for the first sock, the other half of the beads will be for the second sock.) Pass the yarn through the loop of the threader and pick up beads with the working end of the needle.

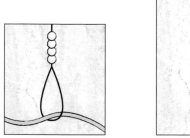

2. Slide the beads over the loop and onto the yarn.

As you work, unwind a small quantity of yarn, each time sliding the beads towards the ball until needed.

Basics Step by Step

Knit (k)

With the yarn in back, insert the tip of the right needle from front to back into the next stitch on the left needle.

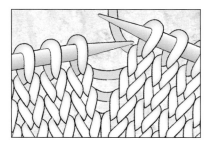

Bring the yarn counterclockwise around the tip of the right needle.

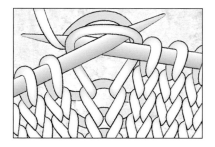

With the point of the right needle, pull the yarn loop through the stitch.

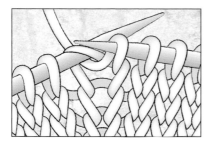

Slide the stitch off the left needle. The new stitch is on the right needle.

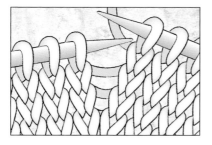

Purl (p)

With the yarn in front, insert the tip of the right needle from back to front through the front loop of the next stitch on the left needle.

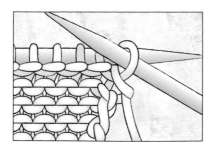

Bring the yarn counterclockwise around the tip of the right needle.

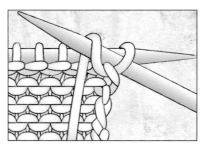

With the point of the right needle, pull the yarn loop through the stitch.

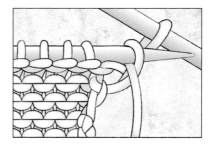

Slide the stitch off the left needle. The new stitch is on the right needle.

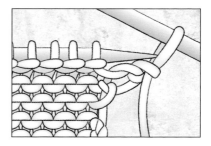

Increase (inc)

Two Stitches in One Stitch

Increase (knit)

Knit the next stitch in the usual manner, but don't remove the stitch from the left needle.

Place the right needle behind the left needle and knit again into the back of the same stitch. Slip the original stitch off the left needle.

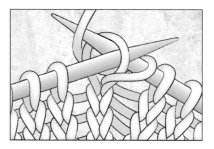

Increase (purl)

Purl the next stitch in the usual manner, but don't remove the stitch from the left needle.

Place the right needle behind the left needle and purl again into the back of the same stitch. Slip the original stitch off the left needle.

Make 1 Increase (m1)

Invisible Increase

Insert the left needle from front to back under the horizontal loop between the last stitch worked and the next stitch on the left needle.

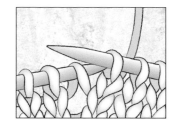

With the right needle, knit into the back of this loop.

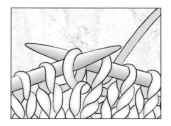

Backward Loop Increase Over the Right Needle

With your thumb, make a loop over the right needle.

Slip the loop from your thumb onto the needle and pull to tighten.

Make 1 Increase in the Top of the Stitch Below

Insert the tip of the right needle into the stitch on left needle one row below.

Knit this stitch, then knit the stitch on the left needle.

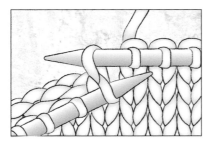

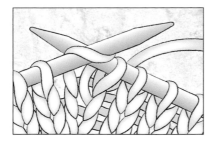

Decrease (dec)

Knit 2 Together (k2tog)

Put the tip of the right needle through the next two stitches on the left needle as if to knit. Knit these two stitches as one.

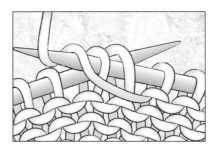

Purl 2 Together (p2tog)

Put the tip of the right needle through next two stitches on the left needle as if to purl. Purl these two stitches as one.

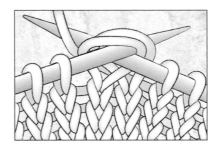

Slip, Slip, Knit (ssk)

Slip the next two stitches, one at a time, from the left needle to right needle as if to knit.

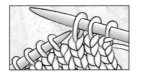 

Insert the left needle in front of both stitches and knit them together as one.

Slip, Slip, Purl (ssp)

Slip the next two stitches, one at a time, from left needle to right needle as if to knit. Slip these stitches back onto the left needle keeping them twisted.

Purl these two stitches together through the back loops.

Crochet Chain

Chain (ch)

Begin by making a slip knot on the hook. Bring the yarn over the hook from back to front, and draw through the loop on the hook.

For each additional chain, bring the yarn over the hook from back to front, and draw through the loop on the hook.

Substituting Yarn

When substituting a different yarn, you should stitch a swatch with the needle/hook size listed to make sure the yarn you have selected matches the gauge given in the pattern.

Changing Needle Size

If you need to stitch *more* stitches in your swatch to create the gauge listed, try the next size *smaller* needle/hook to see if this will give you the correct gauge.

If you need to stitch *fewer* stitches in your swatch to create the gauge listed, try the next size *larger* needle/hook to see if this will give you the gauge.

DETERMINE AMOUNT OF YARN NEEDED		
General conversion amounts for yarns given generically. Yardages are approximations.		
Lace (lace) weight:	1 ounce =	133 yards
Super fine (sock, fingering, baby) weight:	1 ounce =	170–175 yards
Fine (sport) weight:	1 ounce =	90–100 yards
Light (light worsted) weight:	1 ounce =	70–75 yards
Medium (worsted) weight:	1 ounce =	50 yards
Bulky (chunky) weight:	1 ounce =	30–35 yards
Super bulky (super chunky) weight:	1 ounce =	16–23 yards

Basic Stitches

Garter Stitch

When working back and forth, knit every row. When working in the round on circular or double-point needles, knit one round then purl one round.

Stockinette Stitch

When working back and forth, knit the right-side rows, and purl the wrong-side rows. When working in the round on circular or double-point needles, knit all rounds.

Reverse Stockinette Stitch

When working back and forth, purl the right-side rows, and knit the wrong-side rows. When working in the round on circular or double-point needles, purl all rounds.

Ribbing

Ribbing combines knit and purl stitches within a row to give stretch to the garment. Ribbing is most often used for cuffs of hats or socks, but may be used for the entire piece.

The rib pattern is established on the first row. On subsequent rows, the knit stitches are knitted, and the purl stitches are purled to form the ribs.

Reading Pattern Instructions

Before beginning a pattern, read through it to make sure you are familiar with the abbreviations that are used.

Some patterns may be written for more than one size. In this case, the smallest size is given first, and others are placed in parentheses. When only one number is given, it applies to all sizes.

You may wish to highlight the numbers for the size you are making before beginning. It is also helpful to place a self-adhesive sheet on the pattern to note any changes made while working the pattern.

Measuring

To measure pieces, lay them flat on a smooth surface. Take the measurement in the middle of the piece, not along the outer edge where the edges tend to curve or roll.

Gauge

The single most important factor in determining the finished size of a knit item is the gauge. Although not as important for flat, one-piece items, gauge is critical when making a clothing item that needs to fit properly.

It is important to make a stitch gauge swatch of at least 4 inches square using the recommended stitch patterns and needles before beginning.

Block the swatch, then measure it. If the number of stitches and rows in 4 inches is fewer than indicated number under "Gauge" in the pattern, your needles are too large. Try another swatch with smaller needles. If the number of stitches and rows is more than indicated under "Gauge" in the pattern, your needles are too small. Try another swatch with larger needles.

Continue to adjust needles until correct gauge is achieved.

Working From Charts

When working with more than one colour or stitch in a row, sometimes a chart is provided to help follow the pattern. On the chart each square represents one stitch. A key is given indicating the colour or stitch represented by each colour or symbol in the box.

When working in rows, odd-numbered rows are usually read from right to left and even-numbered rows from left to right.

For colour-work charts, rows beginning at the right represent the right side of the work and are usually knit. Rows beginning at the left represent the wrong side and are usually purled.

When working in rounds, every round on the chart is a right-side round, and every round is read from right to left.

Use of Zero

In patterns that include various sizes, zeros are sometimes necessary. For example, k0 (0, 1) means if you are making the smallest or middle size, you would do nothing, and if you are making the largest size, you would k1.

Glossary

bind off—used to finish an edge

cast on—process of making foundation stitches used in knitting

decrease—means of reducing the number of stitches in a row

increase—means of adding to the number of stitches in a row

intarsia—method of knitting a multicoloured pattern into the fabric

knitwise—insert needle into stitch as if to knit

make 1—method of increasing using the strand between the last stitch worked and the next stitch

place marker—placing a purchased marker or loop of contrasting yarn onto the needle for ease in working a pattern repeat

purlwise—insert needle into stitch as if to purl

right side—side of garment or piece that will be seen when worn or used

selvage (selvedge) stitch—edge stitch used to make seaming easier

slip, slip, knit—method of decreasing by moving stitches from left needle to right needle and working them together

slip stitch—an unworked stitch slipped from left needle to right needle, usually as if to purl

wrong side—side that will be inside when garment or piece is worn or used

work even—continue to work in the pattern as established without working any increases or decreases

work in pattern as established—continue to work following the pattern stitch as it has been set up or established on the needle, working any increases or decreases in such a way that the established pattern remains the same

yarn over—method of increasing by wrapping the yarn over the right needle without working a stitch

Standard Abbreviations

[ ] work instructions within brackets as many times as directed
( ) work instructions within parentheses in the place directed
** repeat instructions following the asterisks as directed
* repeat instructions following the single asterisk as directed
" inch(es)

beg begin/beginning
CC contrasting colour
ch chain stitch
cm centimetre(s)
cn cable needle
dec decrease/decreases/decreasing

dpn(s) double-pointed needle(s)
g gram
inc increase/increases/increasing
k knit
k2tog knit 2 stitches together
LH left hand
lp(s) loop(s)
m metre(s)
M1 make one stitch
MC main colour
mm millimetre(s)
oz ounce(s)
p purl
pat(s) pattern(s)
p2tog purl 2 stitches together
pm place marker

psso pass slipped stitch over
p2sso pass 2 slipped stitches over
rem remain/remaining
rep repeat(s)
rev St st reverse stockinette stitch
RH right hand
rnd(s) round(s)
RS right side
skp slip, knit, pass stitch over—one stitch decreased
sk2p slip 1, knit 2 together, pass slip stitch over the knit 2 together—2 stitches have been decreased
sl slip
sl 1k slip 1 knitwise
sl 1p slip 1 purlwise

sl st slip stitch(es)
ssk slip, slip, knit these 2 stitches together—a decrease
st(s) stitch(es)
St st stockinette stitch/ stocking stitch
tbl through back loop(s)
tog together
WS wrong side
wyib with yarn in back
wyif with yarn in front
yd(s) yard(s)
yfwd yarn forward
yo yarn over

Standard Yarn Weight System
Categories of yarn, gauge ranges, and recommended needle sizes

Yarn Weight Symbol & Category Names	1 SUPER FINE	2 FINE	3 LIGHT	4 MEDIUM	5 BULKY	6 SUPER BULKY
Type of Yarns in Category	Sock, Fingering, Baby	Sport, Baby	DK, Light Worsted	Worsted, Afghan, Aran	Chunky, Craft, Rug	Bulky, Roving
Knit Gauge* Ranges in Stockinette Stitch to 4 inches	21–32 sts	23–26 sts	21–24 sts	16–20 sts	12–15 sts	6–11 sts
Recommended Needle in Metric Size Range	2.25–3.25mm	3.25–3.75mm	3.75–4.5mm	4.5–5.5mm	5.5–8mm	8mm
Recommended Needle Canada/U.S. Size Range	1 to 3	3 to 5	5 to 7	7 to 9	9 to 11	11 and larger

* GUIDELINES ONLY: The above reflect the most commonly used gauges and needle sizes for specific yarn categories.

SOCK BASICS

Anatomy of a Sock

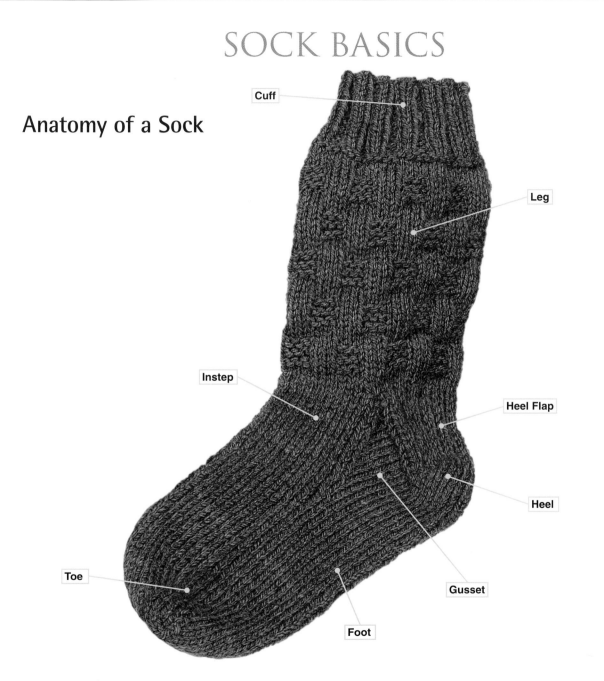

Cuff

Leg

Instep

Heel Flap

Heel

Gusset

Toe

Foot

Cast-On Techniques

For Top-Down Socks

Long-Tail Cast-On

Begin with a length of yarn about three times the length of the finished cast-on edge. Make a slip knot, and place it on the needle. The yarn attached to the ball is the "working end," and the end created from the slip knot is the "long-tail end."

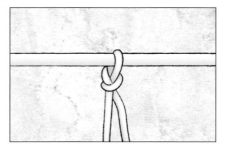

Hold the needle in one hand, and, with the other hand, create a "V" with your thumb and index finger. Hold the long-tail end in the crease of your thumb and the working yarn around your index finger.

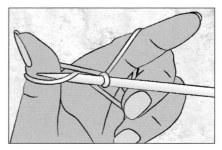

Swing the needle between the opening created under the thumb and the long-tail end, but do not release the yarn in the crease of your thumb.

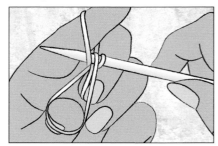

Wrap the working end around the needle, and use your thumb to pull the long-tail end up, over and off the needle as if to knit.

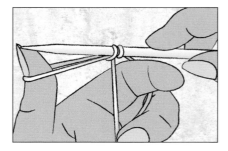

Remove your thumb, and tighten the long-tail end around the base of the stitch.

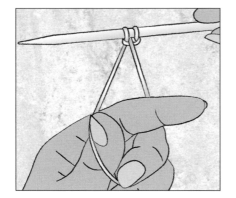

Repeat this process until you have the required number of stitches.

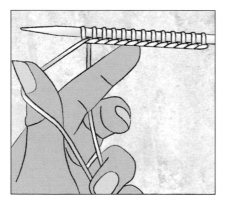

Cable Cast-On

Start with a slip knot placed on the left-hand needle, leaving a short tail. Pick up the right-hand needle, and knit one stitch.

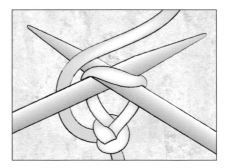

Insert the right-hand needle between the two stitches, wrap the yarn over the needle and draw the yarn through the loop.

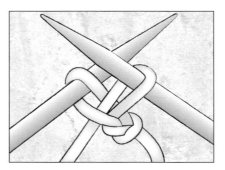

Place the new stitch onto the left-hand needle. Repeat this process until you have the required number of stitches.

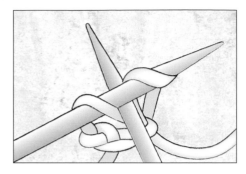

For Toe-Up Socks

Crochet Provisional Cast-On

1. With waste yarn, start by making a slip knot, and place the loop on a crochet hook. *(See page 12 for instructions on making a crochet chain.)*

2. Make a crochet chain long enough to accommodate a few more than the desired number of stitches. Fasten off.

With the knitting needle, pick up one stitch in the back loop of each chain until you have the required number of cast-on stitches. When you are ready to work the live stitches, simply unravel the waste yarn, and place the stitches onto the knitting needle.

Turkish (Figure 8) Cast-On

This is an invisible cast on that forms a closed end. To work the Turkish Cast-On, you need three double-point needles.

1. Hold two needles parallel in your right hand, and wrap the yarn loosely around the needles in a "figure 8" fashion.

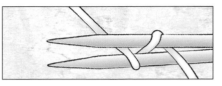

2. Work the "figure 8" up and over both needles until you have the required number of loops on each needle. (The tail end of the yarn will be on the right side.)

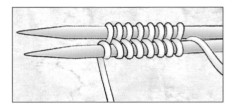

3. With the third needle, knit across the loops on the first needle. Turn.

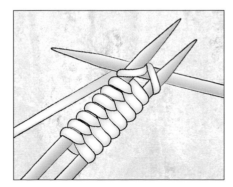

4. Now repeat 3 and knit across the loops on the second needle.

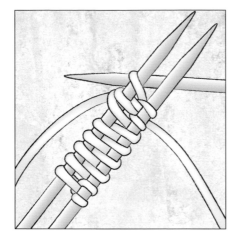

Repeat 3 and 4 until the desired length is reached, alternating needles on each row and increasing stitches as instructed in the pattern text.

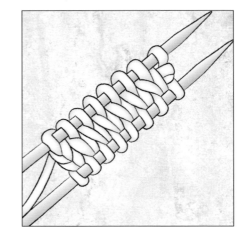

As you continue increasing on either side of the work for toe shaping, a "cup" will begin to form. This will serve as the foundation for your toe.

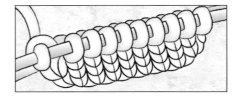

Working in the Round

Working With Double-Point Needles

Notes

Make sure that the cast on edge remains along the inside of the circle on each needle. This will help prevent the stitches from twisting around the needles.

After cast-on row: refer to *Working with Two Circular Needles (see page 22)* to join the first and last stitch.

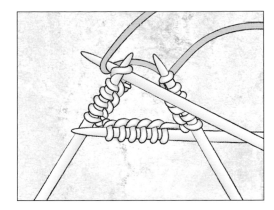

Using 4 Double-Point Needles

Cast on the number of stitches required. Distribute the stitches as instructed in the pattern on 3 double-point needles. Position the needles so that needle 1 is on the left and needle 3 is on the right. The yarn you're about to work with should be attached to the last stitch on needle 3.

Using 5 Double-Point Needles

Cast on the number of stitches required. Distribute stitches evenly on 4 double-point needles. Position the needles so that needle 1 is on the left and needle 4 is on the right. The yarn you're about to work with should be attached to the last stitch on needle 4.

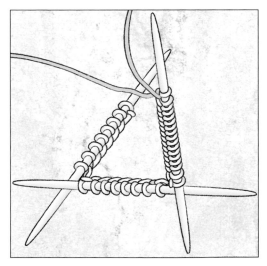

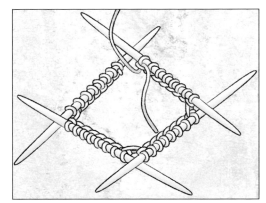

Working With Two Circular Needles

Cast on the required number of stitches onto a circular needle. Slip half of the stitches to a second circular needle. Needle 1 holds the first group of stitches and needle 2 holds the rest of the stitches.

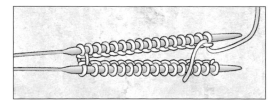

1. Slide all stitches to other end of needles, making sure that needle 2 is on top, and needle 1 is on the bottom.

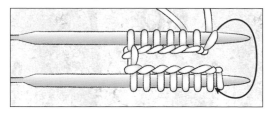

2. Slip the first stitch from needle 1 and place onto needle 2. Slip the ending stitch from needle 2 up and over the stitch just transferred onto needle 1 to "join" into a ring.

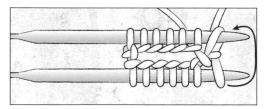

3. Pull needle 1 so the stitches rest on the cable.

4. The working yarn is on needle 2 ready to work. Pick up the other end of needle 2 and work across all stitches.

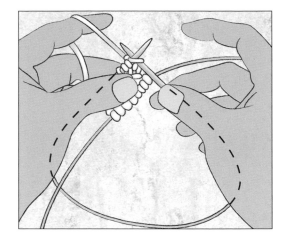

5. Turn the work so needle 1 is ready to work. Pull needle 2, so stitches rest on cable. Pick up opposite end of needle 1 and work across all stitches. Continue in this manner until desired length is reached.

Magic Loop

This method of working in the round uses one long circular needle, ideally one with a very flexible cable. It is very similar to working with two circular needles but many knitters prefer it to working with two needles because it eliminates the distracting loose ends of the second circular needle. Once you master this technique, it's a great solution when working on small-circumference projects.

Cast on or pick up the required number of stitches onto a 29-inch, or longer, circular needle. Slide the stitches to the cable portion of the needle. Pinch the cable in half and then pull to create a large loop. Arrange half the stitches on one needle tip, and half on the other.

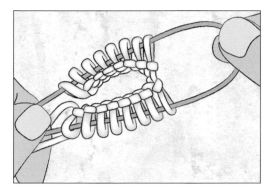

Follow These 3 Easy Steps

1. The illustration above shows how your stitches should look after you have distributed them on the two parts of the needle. The points of the needle and the "tail" from the cast-on row are facing to the right and the cables are on your left.

Tip: After cast-on row: refer to *Working With Two Circular Needles* to join the first and last stitch.

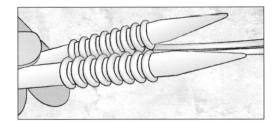

2. The next step, as shown above, illustrates how to begin working your first round: Hold the needle in your left hand, and pull out the needle that holds the "tail end"; the stitches that were on the needle point are now resting on the cable. Begin working the stitches that are still on the opposite needle point as if you were working on straight needles.

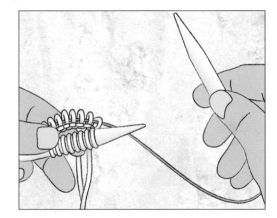

3. At the end of the row, simply turn the work around and reposition the stitches as shown above. Once again, the needles are pointing to the right, and the cable loop is to the left.

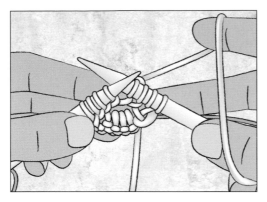

The examples show how the work will appear on the needles as the work gets longer.

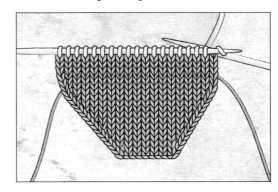

Continue to work in this manner until desired length is reached.

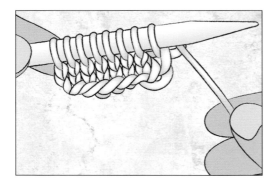

Toes & Heels

Short-Row Toes & Heels

Short rows are partial rows of knitting that are used to create curved sections of knitting. This is a particularly popular method for shaping heels and toes of socks. There are two basic techniques that are often used to close the gaps made by working short rows: wrap and turn and working the wraps.

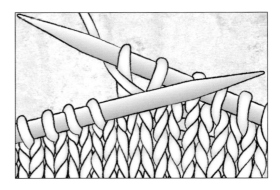

W&T (Wrap and Turn)

On the right side of your work: Bring the yarn to the front of your work between the needles, slip the next stitch to the right-hand needle, move the yarn to the back of your work to "wrap the stitch," slip the stitch back to the left-hand needle, turn and purl back in the other direction.

On the wrong side of your work: Bring the yarn to the back of your work between the needles, slip the next stitch to the right-hand needle, move the yarn to the front of your work to "wrap the stitch," slip the stitch back to the left-hand needle, turn and knit back in the other direction.

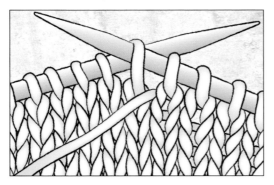

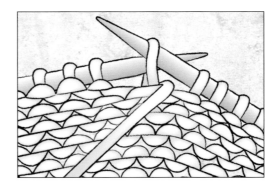

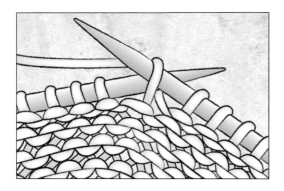

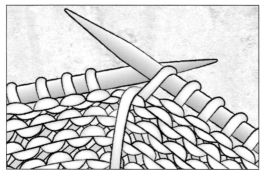

Working Wraps Together With Wrapped Stitches

On the right side of your work: knit to the wrapped stitch. Slip the next stitch from the left-hand needle to the right-hand needle purlwise.

Use the tip of the left-hand needle to pick up the wrap and place it on the right-hand needle. Straighten the stitches out, move them back to the left-hand needle and knit the 2 stitches together.

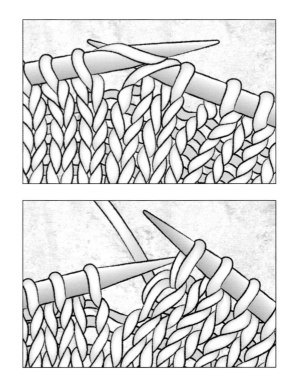

On the wrong side of your work: purl to the wrapped stitch. Slip the next stitch from the left-hand needle to the right-hand needle knitwise. Use the tip of the left-hand needle to pick up the wrap and place it on the right-hand needle.

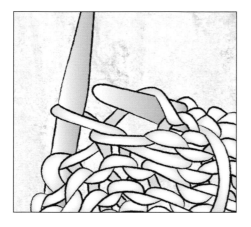

Straighten out the stitches and move them back to the left-hand needle and purl the 2 stitches together through the back loops.

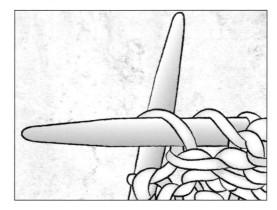

Special Note About Working Wraps

If you're working multiple wraps, there will be a single wrap on the first purl and knit rows. The following rows will have double wraps which will be worked by picking up two wraps instead of one, and then knitting or purling all three stitches together.

Ending the Sock

For Toe-Up Socks

Standard Bind-Off (Knit & Purl)

Binding Off (Knit)

Knit the first two stitches on the left needle. Insert the tip of the left needle into the first stitch worked on the right needle and pull it over the second stitch and completely off the needle.

Knit the next stitch and repeat. When one stitch remains on the right needle, cut the yarn and draw the tail through the last stitch to fasten off.

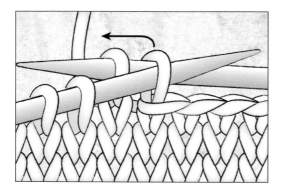

Binding Off (Purl)

Purl the first two stitches on the left needle. Insert the tip of the left needle into the first stitch worked on the right needle and pull it over the second stitch and completely off the needle.

Purl the next stitch and repeat. When one stitch remains on the right needle, cut the yarn and draw the tail through the last stitch to fasten off.

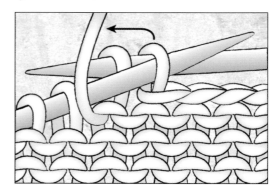

Sewn Bind-Off

Cut a length of yarn, leaving a tail that is about 3 times longer than the diameter of your sock. Thread your tapestry needle.

1. Insert the tapestry needle into the first two stitches purlwise and pull the yarn through.

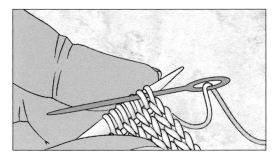

2. Go back and insert the needle knitwise through the first stitch only. Slip this stitch off the knitting needle. Pull the yarn through.

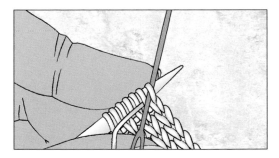

Repeat these two steps until you have bound off all of the stitches.

Stretchy Bind-Off

To use this kind of bind-off, replace one needle with a crochet hook. After each bound-off stitch, chain 1 until all of the stitches are bound off.

For Top-Down Socks

Kitchener Stitch

This method of grafting with two needles is used for the toes of socks and flat seams. To graft the edges together and form an unbroken line of stockinette stitch, divide all of the stitches evenly onto two knitting needles—holding one needle behind the other. Thread the yarn into the tapestry needle. Hold the needles with the wrong sides of the fabric together and work from right to left as follows:

1. Insert the tapestry needle into the first stitch on the front needle as if to purl. Draw the yarn through the stitch, leaving the stitch on the knitting needle.

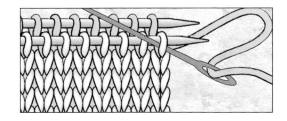

2. Insert the tapestry needle into the first stitch on the back needle as if to purl. Draw the yarn through the stitch and slip the stitch off the knitting needle.

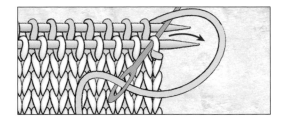

3. Insert the tapestry needle into the next stitch on the same (back) needle as if to knit, leaving the stitch on the knitting needle.

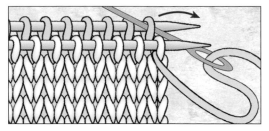

4. Insert the tapestry needle into the first stitch on the front needle as if to knit. Draw the yarn through the stitch and slip the stitch off the knitting needle.

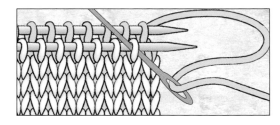

5. Insert the tapestry needle into the next stitch on same (front) needle as if to purl. Draw the yarn through the stitch, leaving the stitch on the knitting needle.

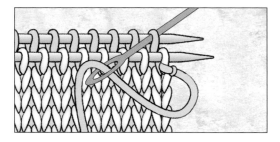

Repeat 2 through 5 until one stitch is left on each needle. Repeat 2 and 4 once more. Fasten off. Grafted stitches should be the same size as the adjacent knitted stitches.

RIBBED ANKLETS

Use self-striping yarn and create anklets that are as individual as you are!

Design | E.J. Slayton

Sizes
Woman's small (medium, large) Instructions are given for smallest size, with larger sizes in parentheses. When only one number is given, it applies to all sizes.

Finished Measurements
Circumference: Approx 8½ (9, 9½) inches
Cuff: Approx 2½ inches high

Materials
Sock weight yarn (414 yds/100g per ball):
   1 ball pink/blue/grey multi
Size 1 (2.25mm) set of 4 double-point needles or size needed to obtain gauge
Stitch marker

Gauge
15 sts and 19 rnds = 2 inches/5cm in St st in rnds.
To save time, take time to check gauge.

Special Abbreviation
N1, N2, N3: Needle 1, Needle 2, Needle 3

Notes
Slip all stitches purlwise with yarn on wrong side of fabric.

Sock may be worked on 2 circular needles, with instep stitches on 1 needle and heel/foot stitches on the other.

Be sure to work each group of stitches with both ends of the same needle; do not work stitches from 1 needle to the other.

For socks that are nearly identical, instead of fraternal twins, start the second sock at the same point in the colour sequence as the first.

Socks

Cuff
Cast on 64 (68, 72) sts, dividing sts onto 3 needles; join without twisting. Mark beg of rnd.

Rnd 1: *K2, p2; rep from * around.

Rep Rnd 1 until cuff measures approx 2½ inches, ending with k2, p2.

Arrange sts with last 32 (34, 36) sts on 1 needle for heel; divide rem sts between 2 needles for instep. There should be a k2 at centre of instep sts.

Heel Flap
Turn and purl across heel sts, inc 1 st at centre back by k1 in top of st in row below st on RH needle—33 (35, 37) sts.

Row 1 (RS): Sl 1, *k1, sl 1; rep from * across.

Row 2: Purl across.

Rep Rows 1 and 2 until there are 16 (17, 18) loops on each edge of heel flap, ending with Row 1.

Turn Heel

Row 1 (WS): P19 (20, 21), p2tog, p1, turn.

Row 2 (RS): Sl 1, k6, k2tog, k1, turn.

Row 3: Sl 1, p7, p2tog, p1, turn.

Row 4: Sl 1, k8, k2tog, k1, turn.

Continue to work as established, having 1 more st before dec every row until all sts have been worked—19 (21, 21) sts rem.

Gusset

With needle containing heel sts, pick up and knit 16 (17, 18) sts in loops along edge of heel flap (N1); work 32 (34, 36) instep sts onto separate needle maintaining pat (optional), and, *at the same time*, at each end, pick up and twist running thread and knit it tog with first and last st (N2); pick up and knit 16 (17, 18) sts along left edge of heel flap, then k9 (10, 10) heel sts onto same needle (N3)—83 (89, 93) sts.

Rnd 1: N1: Knit across; N2: Work in pat across instep sts; N3: Knit across.

Rnd 2: N1: Knit to last 3 sts, k2tog, k1; N2: Work in pat across; N3: K1, ssk, knit to end.

Rnds 3–18 (20, 20): Rep [Rnds 1 and 2] 8 (9, 9) times—65 (69, 73) sts.

Next rnd: Work in established pat around, dec 1 st at beg of rnd—64 (68, 72) sts.

Foot

Continue to work even until foot measures approx 1¾ inches less than desired length. Discontinue instep pat.

Toe

Rnd 1: N1: Knit to last 3 sts, k2tog, k1; N2: K1, ssk, knit to last 3 sts, k2tog, k1; N3: K1, ssk, knit to end.

Rnd 2: Knit around.

Rep Rnds 1 and 2 until 32 (32, 36) sts rem, ending with Rnd 1. Work N1 sts onto N3—16, 16, 18 sts on each of 2 needles.

Cut yarn, leaving an 18-inch end.

Finishing

Weave toe sts tog using Kitchener Stitch (see page 29). ∎

Ribbed Anklets

Sample project was knit with Sockotta (45 per cent cotton/40 per cent superwash wool/15 per cent nylon) from Plymouth Yarn Co.

TREAT FOR YOUR FEET

Try on these toe-up socks as you stitch for the perfect fit.

Design | Christine L. Walter

Sizes

Woman's small (medium) to fit shoe sizes 6–7 (8–9)

Instructions are given for smaller size, with larger size in parentheses. When only one number is given, it applies to both sizes.

Finished Measurements

Circumference: 8¼ (9¼) inches
Foot length: 9 (9¾) inches

Materials

Sport weight yarn (225 yds/100g per skein):
   1 (2) skeins brown (MC) and 1 skein aqua (CC)
Size 2 (2.75mm) double-pointed needles (set of
   5) or size needed to obtain gauge
Spare needle 1–2 sizes larger
Small crochet hook (for Provisional Cast-On)
Stitch marker
Waste yarn
Tapestry needle

2 FINE

Gauge

27 sts and 40 rows = 4 inches/10cm in solid-coloured St st
28 sts and 33 rows = 4 inches/10cm in Two-Colour Pat
To save time, take time to check gauge.

Special Abbreviations

Slip, slip, purl (ssp): [Sl 1 knitwise] twice, pass back to RH needle, p2tog tbl.

Slip, slip, slip, purl (sssp): [Sl 1 knitwise] 3 times, p3tog tbl.

N1, N2, N3, N4: Needle 1, Needle 2, Needle 3, Needle 4.

Pattern Stitch

Two-Colour Pat (multiple of 8 sts)

See chart on page 37.

Special Technique

Provisional Cast-On: With crochet hook and waste yarn, make a chain several sts longer than desired cast on. With knitting needle and project yarn, pick up indicated number of sts in the "bumps" on back of chain. When indicated in pat, "unzip" the crochet chain to free live sts and sl to needle.

Notes

Because feet vary in length, measure your feet and make adjustments as necessary as suggested in the pattern.

Sock circumference should be approximately 10 per cent less than actual foot measurement; allowing for "negative ease" and a snug, non-slouchy fit.

Treat for Your Feet
Sample project was knit with Gems Sport (100 per cent merino wool) from Louet.

On foot, N1 and N2 hold instep stitches; N3 and N4 hold sole stitches. On cuff, beginning of round is at centre back.

When working Two-Colour Pat, be careful to carry yarn not in use very loosely on wrong side to ensure fabric elasticity.

To ensure a very loose bind off, use a needle 1 or 2 sizes larger to bind off.

Socks
Using Provisional Cast-On method (see page 19) and MC, cast on 28 (32) sts.

Knit 1 row.

Short-Row Toe
Row 1 (RS): Knit to last st, turn, leaving last st on needle.

Row 2: Wyib, yo, then purl to last st, turn, leaving last st on needle.

Row 3: Yo, knit to 1 st before the paired st/yo of the previous row, turn.

Row 4: Wyib, yo, purl to 1 st before the paired st/yo of previous row, turn.

Continue working in this manner, starting each row with a yo and ending with 1 st less than before until you have 10 (12) sts between yo's. The last turn will bring you to a RS row.

Next row (RS): Yo, knit to the first yo; sl yo purlwise onto the RH hand needle, then return it to the LH needle by inserting the needle from front to back (this reverses the way the yo is mounted), k2tog, turn.

Row 5: Yo, purl to the first yo, ssp, turn.

Row 6: Yo, knit to the first yo. (There are 2 yo's side by side.) Sl both yo's purlwise 1 at a time to the RH needle, then return them to the LH needle as before by inserting the needle from front to back, k3tog, turn.

Row 7: Yo, purl to the first yo on the next needle. Again you find 2 yo's side by side, sssp, turn.

Rep last 2 rows until all yo's of the toe have been consumed in the dec. Turn.

Foot
Set-up rnd: N1: yo, k14 (16); N2: knit to last yo. Carefully unzip the Provisional Cast-On st by st and sl 14 (16) sts each to N3 and N4. You should have 15 (17) sts on N1 and N2 [each needle has 1 yo plus 14 (16) sts] and 14 (16) sts on each of N3 and N4. N3: sl the yo at the end of N2 to the beg of N3 and k2tog, k13 (15); N4: k13 (15), ssk the last st from N4 with the yo at the beg of N1; place marker for beg of rnd—56 (64) sts; 14 (16) sts on each dpn.

Rnd 1: P1, [k2, p2] 6 (7) times, k2, p1, k28 (32).

Rep Rnd 1 until sock measures 7 (7¾) inches from beg or 2 inches less than desired length of foot to heel.

Short-Row Heel
Sl sts on N1 and N2 to 1 dpn for heel, sl sts on N3 and N4 to single dpn for holder.

Work short row heel as for short row toe, then continue as follows:

Next rnd (RS): N4: Yo, k14 (16), place marker for beg of rnd; N1: knit to last yo, transfer the yo to the dpn with sts on hold; N2: k2tog (yo and first st), k13 (15); N3: k13 (15), sl the yo from end of N4 and ssk the last st with the yo; N4: knit—56 (64) sts.

Cuff

Work in Two-Colour Pat for 39 (42) rnds or to desired length. Do not cut yarns.

Cuff Edge

Rnd 1: Knit with CC.

Rnd 2: Purl with CC.

Rnd 3: *K1 MC, k1 CC; rep from * around.

Rnd 4: *P1 MC, k1 CC; rep from * around.

Rep Rnds 1 and 2 once more.

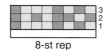

8-st rep

Two-Colour Chart

COLOUR KEY
- MC
- CC

Bind off using two-colour bind-off method as follows: K1 CC, k1 MC, pass first st over 2nd st; continue binding off in this manner working each st in alternating colour.

Cut yarn, leaving an 8-inch tail.

Finishing

Weave in ends. Block lightly. ∎

3 & 1 SLIP-STITCH SOCKS

Brighten your day and your sandals with a colourful pair of socks.

Design | E.J. Slayton

Sizes
Woman's small (medium, large) Instructions are given for smallest size, with larger sizes in parentheses. When only one number is given, it applies to all sizes.

Finished Measurements
Cuff: 7 (7, 8) inches
Foot length: 8 (9, 10) inches

Materials
Worsted weight yarn (245 yds/100g per skein):
   1 (1, 2) skeins natural (MC), 1 skein each pink
   (A), sapphire (B), and navy (C)
Size 3 (3.25mm) needles or size needed to obtain gauge
Size 4 (3.5mm) double-pointed needles
Stitch markers
Stitch holder
Tapestry needle

Gauge
12 sts and 16 rnds = 2 inches/5 cm in St st on smaller
   needles
To save time, take time to check gauge.

Special Abbreviation
N1, N2, N3: Needle 1, Needle 2, Needle 3

Pattern Stitches
3 & 1 Slip Stitch (multiple of 4 sts)

Rnd 1: With CC, *sl 1, k3; rep from * around.

Rnd 2: With CC, *sl 1, p3; rep from * around.

Rnds 3 and 4: With MC, k2, *sl 1, k3; rep from * around, end last rep sl 1, k1.

Rep Rnds 1–4 for pat.

Colour Sequence
Rnds 1–4: Work with A.

Rnds 5–8: Work with B.

Rnds 9–12: Work with C.

Rep Rnds 1–12 for colour sequence.

Notes
When working pattern, slip all stitches purlwise with yarn on wrong side of fabric.

Sock is shown with pattern extending to bottom of heel, suitable for wearing with sandals or clogs.

Alternate instructions are included for a plain heel.

3 & 1 Slip-Stitch Socks
Sample project was knit with Nature Spun
(100 per cent wool) from Brown Sheep Co. Inc.

Socks

Cuff
With MC and smaller needles, cast on 40 (44, 48) sts. Divide sts on 3 needles and join, being careful not to twist. Work in K2, P2 Rib for 2 inches.

Leg
Change to larger needles.

Knit 2 rnds.

Beg with A, work in 3 & 1 Slip St pat and Colour Sequence until leg measures 7 (7, 8) inches or desired length to heel, ending with Rnd 4 of pat.

Size Medium Only
Work first st of next rnd onto last needle.

Choose your style of heel, either patterned or plain.

Heel

Patterned Heel
Note: Sl first and last st of every WS row.

Work across next 21 (23, 25) sts for heel, sl rem 19 (21, 23) sts to holder. Work in rows from this point.

Row 1: With next CC in sequence, k4 (3, 4), *sl 1, k3; rep from * to last 5 (4, 5) sts, end last rep sl 1, k4 (3, 4).

Row 2: Sl 1, k3 (2, 3), *sl 1, k3; rep from * to last 5 (4, 5) sts, end last rep sl 1, k3 (2, 3), sl 1.

Row 3: With MC, k2 (1, 2), *sl 1, k3; rep from * to last 3 (2, 3) sts, end last rep sl 1, k2 (1, 2).

Row 4: With MC, sl 1, p1 (0, 1), *sl 1, p3; rep from * to last 3 (2, 3) sts, end last rep sl 1, p1 (0, 1), sl 1.

Rows 5–20 (24, 24): Rep [Rows 1–4] 4 (5, 5) times. Cut CC and work with MC from this point.

Next row: With MC, knit across.

Continue with turn heel below.

Plain Heel
Divide for heel as for patterned heel, work with MC throughout.

Row 1 (RS): Sl 1, *k1, sl 1; rep from * across.

Row 2: Purl.

Rows 3–18 (22, 22): Rep [Rows 1 and 2] 8 (10, 10) times.

Row 19 (23, 23): Rep Row 1–10 (12, 12) loops on each side of heel flap.

Continue with turn heel below.

Turn Heel
Place marker in st 11 (12, 13) for centre of heel. Shaping takes place evenly spaced on each side of this centre st.

Row 1 (WS): Sl 1, p12 (13, 14), p2tog, p1, turn.

Row 2: Sl 1, k6, k2tog, k1, turn.

Row 3: Sl 1, p7, p2tog, p1, turn.

Row 4: Sl 1, k8, k2tog, k1, turn.

Continue to work in this manner, having 1 more st before dec on each row until all sts have been worked, ending with a RS row—13 (15, 15) heel sts.

Work in rnds from this point.

Rnd 1: Knit.

Rnd 2: N1: Knit to last 3 sts, k2tog, k1; N2: Knit across; N3: K1, ssk, knit to end.

Rep Rnds 1 and 2 until 38 (42, 46) sts rem.

Foot
Work even in St st until foot measures 7½ (8, 8½) inches or approximately 2 inches less than desired length.

Toe
Rnd 1: Knit.

Rnd 2: N1: Knit to last 3 sts, k2tog, k1; N2: K1, ssk, knit to last 3 sts, k2tog, k1; N3: K1, ssk, knit to end.

Rep Rnds 1 and 2 until 22 sts rem for all sizes.

With N3, knit across sts of N1—11 sts each on 2 needles. Cut yarn, leaving an 18-inch end.

Finishing
Weave toe sts tog using Kitchener Stitch (see page 29). ■

Gussett
Change to smaller needles. With N1, pick up and knit 10 (12, 12) sts in loops along left edge of heel flap; with N2 knit across 19 (21, 23) instep sts on holder; with N3 pick up and knit 10 (12, 12) sts in loops along right edge of heel flap, knit 6 (7, 7) heel sts; sl rem 7 (8, 8) heel sts onto N1—52 (60, 62) sts [17 (20, 20) sts on N1, 19 (21, 23) sts on N2, and 16 (19, 19) sts on N3].

FANCY LACE SOCKS

Add flair to any outfit with these textured lace socks.

Design | Fran Ortmeyer

Sizes
Adult's small (medium, large) Instructions are given for smallest size, with larger sizes in parentheses. When only one number is given, it applies to all sizes.

Finished Measurements
Circumference: 7½ (8½, 9½) inches
Foot length: Make to desired length.

Materials
Sport weight yarn (168 yds/70g per ball):
   2 balls lime
Size 5 (3.75mm) double-point needles *for size small*;
   Size 6 (4mm) double-point needles *for size medium*;
   Size 7 (4.5mm) double-point needles *for size large*, or size needed to obtain gauge
2 ring-type stitch markers
Stitch holder

Gauge
24 sts = 3 inches/7.5cm in St st on size 5 needles.
28 sts = 4 inches/10cm in St st on size 6 needles.
25 sts = 4 inches/10cm in St st on size 7 needles.

Special Abbreviations
N1, N2, N3: Needle 1, Needle 2, Needle 3

Slip, knit, pass (skp): Slip next st, k1, pass slipped stitch over knit st to dec 1 st.

Notes
Instructions are the same for all sizes, sock size is determined by needle size.

Slip all stitches purlwise with yarn on wrong side of work unless otherwise stated.

Socks

Cuff
Working loosely, cast 16 sts on each of 3 needles; join being careful not to twist—48 sts.

Rnd 1: *K2, p2; rep from * around.

Rnds 2–15: Rep Rnd 1.

Leg
Rnd 1: *K5, p2, k3, p2; rep from * around.

Rnds 2 and 3: Rep Rnd 1.

Rnd 4: *K2tog, yo, k1, yo, skp, p2, k2tog, yo, k1, p2; rep from * around.

Rnds 5–7: *K5, p2, k3, p2; rep from * around.

Rnd 8: *K2tog, yo, k1, yo, skp, p2, k1, yo, k2tog, p2; rep from * around.

Rep Rnds 1–8 until piece measures approx 8 inches from cast-on edge, ending with a Rnd 4 or Rnd 8.

Heel Flap

Row 1: Working on 1 needle, (sl 1, k1) 12 times—24 sts. Place rem 24 sts on holder for instep.

Row 2: Sl 1, p23, turn.

Row 3: *Sl 1, k1; rep from * across, turn.

Rows 4–19: Rep [Rows 2 and 3] 8 times.

Row 20: Rep Row 2.

Mark Row 20 for base of Heel.

Turn Heel

Row 1: Sl 1, k12, skp, k1, turn, leaving last 8 sts unworked—23 sts on needle.

Row 2: Sl 1, p3, p2 tog, p1, turn, leaving last 8 sts unworked—22 sts.

Fancy Lace Socks
Sample project was knit with Microspun (100 per cent microfibre acrylic) from Lion Brand Yarn Co.

Row 3: Sl 1, k4, skp, k1, turn, leaving last 6 sts unworked—21 sts.

Row 4: Sl 1, p5, p2 tog, p1, turn, leaving last 6 sts unworked—20 sts.

Row 5: Sl 1, k6, skp, k1, turn, leaving last 4 sts unworked—19 sts.

Row 6: Sl 1, p7, p2tog, p1, turn, leaving last 4 sts unworked—18 sts.

Row 7: Sl 1, k8, skp, k1, turn, leaving last 2 sts unworked—17 sts.

Row 8: Sl 1, p9, p2 tog, p1, turn, leaving last 2 sts unworked—16 sts.

Row 9: Sl 1, k10, skp, p1, turn—15 sts.

Row 10: Sl 1, p11, p2 tog, p1, turn—14 sts.

Row 11: Knit next 14 sts of heel; do not turn. Cut yarn.

Gusset

Set-up rnd: With N1, pick up and knit 10 sts evenly spaced in ends of rows along side of heel flap, knit first 7 sts of heel; with N2, knit next 7 sts of heel, pick up and knit 10 evenly spaced in ends of rows along other side of heel flap; with N3, knit next 24 unworked sts; do not turn—58 sts on needles.

Rnd 1: N1: Skp, knit across; N2, knit to last 2 sts, k2tog; N3; knit—56 sts.

Rnd 2: Knit around.

Rnds 3–12: Rep [Rnds 1 and 2] 5 times—46 sts on needles.

Next rnd: Redistribute sts as follows: N1: K16; N2: k15; N3: k15.

Foot

Measure the length of foot that will wear these socks from base of heel to tip of toe.

Continue in St st until piece measures 2 inches less than desired length of foot.

Toe

Rnd 1: [K2tog, k17, skp, k1, place marker, k1] twice—42 sts.

Rnd 2: Knit around, slipping markers as you come to them.

Rnd 3: [K2 tog, knit to 3 sts before next marker, skp, k2] twice—38 sts.

Rnds 4–13: Rep [Rnds 2 and 3] 5 times—18 sts at end of last rnd.

Sl first 8 sts onto one needle; sl rem 9 sts onto separate needle, sl last st onto first needle—9 sts on each of 2 needles. Cut yarn, leaving an 18-inch end.

Finishing

Weave toe sts tog using Kitchener Stitch (see page 29). ■

SIMPLE SELF-STRIPING SOCKS

Complement any outfit with these casual socks. The pattern can be used to make socks for men as well.

Design | Kate Atherley

Sizes
Woman's small (woman's large, man's small, man's large) to fit woman's shoe sizes 5–7 (7½–9) and man's shoe sizes 6–9 (9½–11) Instructions are given for smallest size, with larger sizes in parentheses. When only one number is given, it applies to all sizes.

Finished Measurements
Circumference: 7½ (8, 8½, 9) inches
Foot length: 9 (10, 10, 11) inches

Materials
Sock weight yarn (186 yds/50g per ball): 2 balls dark pinks/light blues

Size 1 (2.25 mm) double-pointed needles (set of 4) or size needed to obtain gauge
Stitch markers, 1 in CC for beg of rnd

Gauge
30 sts and 42 rnds = 4 inches/10cm in St st.
To save time, take time to check gauge.

Special Abbreviation
N1, N2, N3: Needle 1, Needle 2, Needle 3

Note
This sock is worked on 3 double-point needles from the cuff down, with a heel flap, gusset and a wedge toe.

Socks

Leg
Cast on 56 (60, 64, 68) sts. Distribute evenly on 3 dpns; place marker for beg of rnd and join, taking care not to twist sts.

Work K2, P2 Rib for 2 inches.

Change to St st and work even until leg measures 6 (6½, 7½, 8) inches.

Heel
Row 1 (RS): K14 (15, 15, 17), turn.

Row 2: P28 (30, 32, 34), turn, leaving rem 28 (30, 32, 34) sts on hold on dpns for instep.

Row 3: Sl 1, knit across heel sts.

Row 4: Sl 1, purl across heel sts.

Rep [Rows 3 and 4] 8 (9, 10, 11) times.

Turn Heel
Row 1 (RS): Sl 1, k18 (19, 20, 22), ssk, turn.

Row 2: Sl 1, p10 (10, 10, 12), p2tog, turn.

Row 3: Sl 1, k10 (10, 10, 12), ssk, turn.

Rep Rows 2 and 3 until all sts have been worked, ending with a WS row—12 (12, 12, 14) sts.

Gusset

Set-up rnd: With N1, sl 1, knit across heel sts, then pick up and knit 14 (15, 16, 17) sts along left side of flap; with N2, knit across instep sts; with N3, pick up and knit 14 (15, 16, 17) sts along right side of flap, then k6 (6, 6, 7) sts from N1. Place marker for beg of rnd in centre of heel—68 (72, 76, 82) sts distributed as follows: 20 (21, 22, 24) sts on both N1 and N3; 28 (30, 32, 34) sts on N2.

Rnd 1: Knit around, knitting into back loop of all picked-up sts.

Rnd 2 (dec): N1: Knit to last 3 sts, k2tog, k1; N2: knit across; N3: k1, ssk, knit to end.

Rnd 3: Knit around.

Rep Rnds 2 and 3 until 56 (60, 64, 68) sts rem with 14 (15, 16, 17) sts on N1 and N3.

Foot

Work even until foot measures 7 (8, 8, 9) inches or approx 2 inches short of desired length.

Toe

Dec rnd: N1: Knit to last 3 sts, k2tog, k1; N2: k1, ssk, knit to last 3 sts, k2tog, k1; N3: k1, ssk, knit to end—52 (56, 60, 64) sts.

Rep Dec rnd [every 4 rnds] once, [every 3 rnds] twice, [every other rnd] 3 times, then every rnd until 8 sts rem.

Cut yarn, leaving a 6-inch tail.

Using tapestry needle, thread tail through rem sts, and pull tight and secure on WS.

Finishing

Weave in all ends. Block. ■

Simple Self-Striping Socks
Sample project was knit with Echo (45 per cent cotton/40 per cent superwash wool/15 per cent nylon) from Premier Yarns.

UNDULATIONS SOCKS

Use a fingering weight for these easy-to-make, perfect-fit socks for any size!

Design | Amy Polcyn

Sizes

Woman's small (medium, large, extra-large) to fit shoe sizes 6–6½ (7–7½, 8–8½, 9–9½) Instructions are given for smallest size, with larger sizes in parentheses. When only one number is given, it applies to all sizes. When two numbers are given, the smaller is for a narrow/medium foot and the larger is for a wider foot.

Finished Measurements

Circumference: 8 (9½) inches
Foot length: 8¾ (9, 9¼, 9¾) inches

Materials

Sock weight yarn (465 yds/100g per ball):
   1 ball pink
Size 1 (2.5mm) double-point needles (set of 5) or size needed to obtain gauge
Small crochet hook (for Provisional Cast-On)
Spare needle 1 or 2 sizes larger
Waste yarn
Stitch marker
Tapestry needle

1 SUPER FINE

Gauge

30 sts and 46 rows = 4 inches/10cm in St st
To save time, take time to check gauge.

Special Abbreviation

N1, N2, N3, N4: Needle 1, Needle 2, Needle 3, Needle 4

Special Techniques

Provisional Cast-On: With crochet hook and waste yarn, make a chain several sts longer than desired cast on. With knitting needle and project yarn, pick up indicated number of sts in the "bumps" on back of chain. When indicated in pat, "unzip" the crochet chain to free live sts.

Wrap and Turn: Move yarn between needles to RS, sl next st, move yarn back to WS, turn piece, sl st back to other needle.

Pattern Stitch

Undulation Pat (multiple of 6 sts)

Rnds 1 and 2: *P4, k2; rep from * to end.

Rnds 3 and 4: *P3, k3; rep from * to end.

Rnds 5 and 6: *P2, k4; rep from * to end.

Rnds 7 and 8: *P1, k4, p1; rep from * to end.

Rnds 9 and 10: *P1, k3, p2; rep from * to end.

Rnds 11 and 12: *P1, k2, p3; rep from * to end.

Rep Rnds 1–12 for pat.

Notes

Work length appropriate for shoe size. Smaller stitch count is for narrow/medium width foot; larger stitch count is for wide foot.

Undulations Socks

Sample project was knit with TOFUtsies (50 per cent superwash wool/25 per cent Soysilk/22½ per cent cotton/2½ per cent chitin) from South West Trading Co.

Sock circumference should be approximately 10 per cent less than actual foot measurement allowing for "negative ease" and a snug, non-slouchy fit.

To ensure a very loose bind off, use a needle 1 or 2 sizes larger to bind off.

Needle 1 and Needle 4 hold sole stitches; Needle 2 and Needle 3 hold instep stitches.

Chart for Undulations stitch pattern is given on next page for those preferring to work pattern stitch from a chart.

Socks

Using Provisional Cast-On method and single dpn, cast on 30 (36) sts.

Purl 1 row.

Short-Row Toe
Row 1 (RS): Knit to last st, wrap and turn.

Row 2: Purl to last st, wrap and turn.

Row 3: Knit to st before last wrapped st, wrap and turn.

Row 4: Purl to st before last wrapped st, wrap and turn.

Rep Rows 3 and 4 until 9 (10) sts are wrapped on each side, leaving 12 (16) sts unworked in centre of row. Half of the toe is complete.

Next row (RS): Knit to first wrapped st, knit st tog with wrap, wrap and turn. (Next st will now have 2 wraps—on subsequent rows knit wrapped st tog with both wraps.)

Next row: Purl to first wrapped st, purl st tog with wrap, wrap and turn. (Next st will now have 2 wraps—on subsequent rows, knit wrapped st tog with both wraps.)

Rep last 2 rows until all sts have been worked and no wraps rem. Toe is complete.

Foot
Set-up rnd: N4: k15 (18), place marker for beg of rnd; N1: k15 (18); carefully unzip the Provisional Cast-On st by st and sl 15 (18) sts each to N2 and N3; pick up a running thread between N1 and N2, and with N1, knit it tbl; N2 and N3: knit; N4: pick up a running thread between N3 and N4 and knit it tbl, knit to end—62 (74) sts.

Rnd 1: N1: knit to last 2 sts, k2tog; N2 and N3: work in pat; N4: ssk, knit to end—60 (72) sts.

Continue working St st on N1 and N4 and work Undulation Pat on N2 and N3 until sock measures 7 (7¼, 7½, 8) inches or approx 1¾ inches less than desired length, ending with N3.

Short-Row Heel
Sl sts on N4 and N1 to 1 dpn for heel, keeping sts on N2 and N3 on hold.

Work short row heel as for short row toe.

Leg
Continue in the rnd, work Undulation pat on all sts until leg measures 6 inches or desired length.

Work in K2, P2 Rib for 1 inch.

Bind off very loosely in rib.

Finishing
Weave in ends, block if desired. ∎

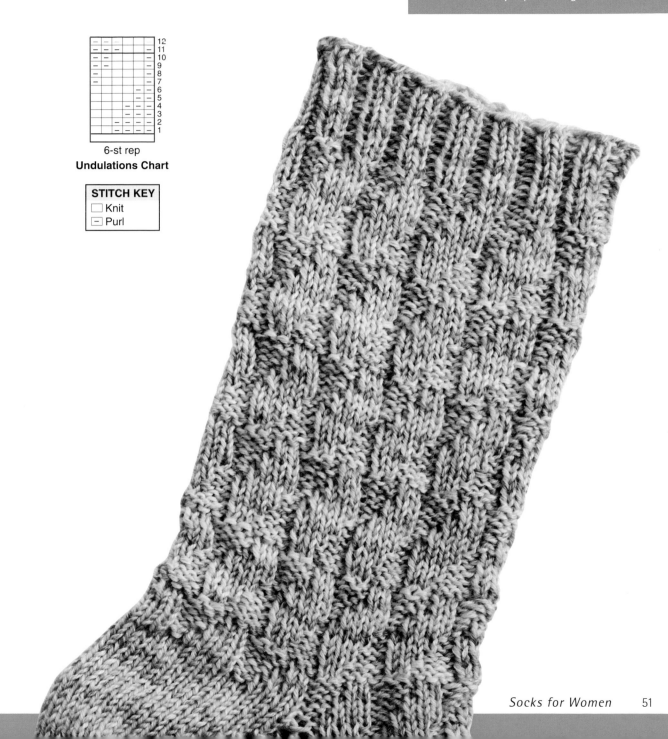

						12
−	−				−	11
−	−	−			−	10
−	−				−	9
−	−				−	8
−					−	7
			−		−	6
			−		−	5
		−	−		−	4
		−	−		−	3
	−	−			−	2
	−	−	−		−	1

6-st rep
Undulations Chart

STITCH KEY
☐ Knit
− Purl

TWISTED RIB SOCKS

Get two looks in one with these reversible socks. This easy-to-memorize pattern will compliment any wardrobe.

Design | Kathryn Beckerdite

Sizes

Woman's small (woman's large, man's small, man's large) to fit woman's shoe size 6–7 (woman's 8–9, man's shoe size 8–9, man's 10–11) Instructions are given for smallest size, with larger sizes in parentheses. When only one number is given, it applies to all sizes.

Finished Measurements

Circumference: 7½ (8, 8½, 9) inches
Foot length: 9 (9¾, 10½, 11 ¼) inches

Materials

Sock weight yarn (215 yds/50g per skein):
  3 (3, 4, 4) skeins rust (MC); 1 skein green (CC)
Size 1 (2.25mm) double-point needles (set of 5) or size
  needed to obtain gauge
Stitch marker
Small crochet hook (for Provisional Cast-On)

Gauge

36 sts and 44 rnds = 4 inches/10cm in St st.
To save time, take time to check gauge.

Special Abbreviations

N1, N2, N3, N4: Needle 1, Needle 2, Needle 3, Needle 4

Wrap and Turn (W&T): Bring yarn to RS of work between needles, slip next st pwise to RH needle, bring yarn around this st to WS, slip st back to LH needle, turn work to begin working back in the other direction.

Work wrapped sts and wraps tog (WW): *On RS:* Knit to wrapped st, slip the wrapped st purlwise from LH needle to RH needle. Use tip of LH needle to pick up wrap(s) and place it/them on RH needle. Slip wrap(s) and st back to LH needle and knit them tog. *On WS:* Purl to wrapped st, slip the wrapped st knitwise from LH needle to RH needle. Use tip of LH to pick up wrap(s) and place it/them on RH needle. Slip wrap(s) and st back to LH needle and purl them tog.

Make 1 (M1): Insert LH needle from front to back under the running thread between the last st worked and next st on LH needle. With RH needle, knit into the back of this loop.

Right Twist (RT): K2tog but do not drop sts from LH needle, knit again into first st on LH needle, drop both sts from LH needle.

Left Twist (LT): Bring RH needle behind LH needle and knit into back of 2nd st on LH needle without dropping st from needle; knit into front of first st on LH needle, drop both stitches from LH needle.

Twisted Rib Socks
Sample project was knit with Wildfoote
Luxury Sock (75 per cent washable wool/
25 per cent nylon) from Brown Sheep Co. Inc.

Pattern Stitch

Twisted Rib (multiple of 5 sts)

Rnd 1: *P1, RT, p1, k1; rep from * to end.

Rnds 2–4: *P1, k2, p1, k1; rep from * to end.

Rep Rnds 1–4 for pat for first sock.

On 2nd sock, work LT instead of RT.

Special Techniques

Provisional Cast-On: With crochet hook and waste yarn, make a chain several sts longer than desired cast on. With knitting needle and project yarn, pick up indicated number of sts in the "bumps" on back of chain. When indicated in pat, "unzip" the crochet chain to free live sts.

Sewn Bind-Off: Cut yarn leaving a 1-yd tail. Using a tapestry needle, *thread the yarn pwise through the first 2 sts on the needle. Pull through, leaving the sts on the needle. Thread the yarn kwise through the first st on the needle, pull through. Drop the first st off the needle. Rep from * around.

Notes

These socks are worked on 4 double-pointed needles from the toe up with short-row toe and heel shaping and ending with a Sewn Bind-Off.

Instep stitches are on Needle 1 and Needle 2; sole stitches are on Needle 3 and Needle 4.

First Sock

Short-Row Toe

Using provisional method and MC, cast on 36 (40, 44, 48) sts.

Row 1 (WS): Purl.

Row 2: Knit to last st, W&T.

Row 3: Purl to last st, W&T.

Row 4: Knit to st before last wrapped st, W&T.

Row 5: Purl to st before last wrapped st, W&T.

Rep Rows 4 and 5 until 14 (16, 18, 20) sts rem unwrapped.

Row 6 (RS): Purl to the first wrapped st, WW, W&T.

Row 7: Knit to the first wrapped st, WW, W&T.

Row 8: Purl to the first double-wrapped st, WW, W&T.

Row 9: Knit to the first double-wrapped st, WW, W&T.

Rep Rows 8 and 9 until 2 double-wrapped sts rem (1 at each end).

Row 10 (RS): Purl across, WW, place marker for beg of rnd.

Unzip Provisional Cast-On and distribute newly live (instep) sts and sole sts evenly divided on 4 dpns—72 (80, 88, 96) sts with 18 (20, 22, 24) sts on each needle.

Foot Instep

Rnd 1 (inc instep sts): N1 and N2: [K4, M1] 8 (9, 10, 11) times, k4; N3 and N4: WW last double-wrapped st, purl to end of rnd—80 (89, 99, 107) sts with 44 (49, 54, 59) sts on N1 and N2 and 36 (40, 44, 48) sts on N3 and N4.

Rnd 2 (set-up rnd): N1 and N2: [P1, RT, p1, k1] 8 (9, 10, 11) times, p1, RT, p1; N3 and N4: purl to end of rnd.

Work even in established pats (Twisted Rib on N1 and N2 and rev St st on N3 and N4) until piece measures 7 (7½, 8¼, 8¾) inches or approx 2 (2¼, 2¼, 2½) inches short of desired length and ending with Rnd 2 of Twisted Rib; turn after completing last rnd.

Heel

Row 1 (WS): K36 (40, 44, 48), turn, leaving instep sts on hold on N1 and N2.

Row 2 (RS): Purl to last st, W&T.

Row 3: Knit to last st, W&T.

Row 4: Purl to st before last wrapped st, W&T.

Row 5: Knit to st before last wrapped st, W&T.

Rep Rows 4 and 5 until 14 (16, 18, 20) sts rem unwrapped.

Row 6: Purl to the first wrapped st, WW, W&T.

Row 7: Knit to the first wrapped st, WW, W&T.

Row 8: Purl to the first double-wrapped st, WW, W&T.

Row 9: Knit to the first double-wrapped st, pick up wraps, WW, W&T.

Rep Rows 8 and 9 until 2 double-wrapped sts rem (1 at each end).

Row 10: Purl to double-wrapped st, WW, do not turn.

Leg

Rnd 1: N1 and N2: Work in established rib; N3 and N4: WW, purl to end.

Rnd 2 (inc): N1 and N2: Work in cstablishcd rib; N3 and N4: [M1, p1, k2, p1] 9 (10, 11, 12) times, end M1—90 (100, 110, 120) sts with 44 (49, 54, 59) sts on N2 and N2 and 46 (51, 56, 61) sts on N3 and N4.

Work even in established Twisted Rib all around until leg measures approx 11¾ (12¼, 13½, 14¼) inches or desired length to cuff.

Cuff

Change to CC and continue in Twisted Rib for approx 2½ (3, 4, 4¼) inches or desired length of cuff, ending with Rnd 4.

Work Rnd 2 once more.

Finishing

Bind off using sewn bind-off. Weave in ends.

Second Sock

Make a 2nd sock, substituting LT for RT in Twisted Rib. ■

SOCKS WITH A TWINKLE

These lovely cotton socks are embellished with complementary shades of sparkling beads, adding a little elegance to your feet.

Design | Christine L. Walter

Size
Woman's small/medium

Finished Measurement
Circumference: Approx 8 inches

Materials
Sport weight yarn (414 yds/100g per ball):
  1 ball purple/brown multi
Size 2 (2.75mm) double-point needles (set of 5) or size needed to obtain gauge
Size 6/0 seed beads: 50 each in crystal silver lined (A), fuchsia silver lined (B), crystal yellow lined (C) and crystal hot pink lined (D), or colours of your choice
Beading needle

Gauge
32 sts and 42 rnds = 4 inches/10 cm in St st.
To save time, take time to check gauge.

Special Abbreviations
BUB (Bring Up Bead): Slide a bead up against the stitch just worked (see page 8).

N1, N2, N3, N4: Needle 1, Needle 2, Needle 3, Needle 4

Pattern Stitch
Beaded Rib (multiple of 12 sts)

Rnds 1 and 2: *K2, p2; rep from * around.

Rnd 3: *[K2, p2] twice, k2, p1, BUB, p1; rep from * around.

Rnds 4–6: Rep Rnd 1.

Rnd 7: *K2, p1, BUB, p1, [k2, p2] twice; rep from * around.

Rnds 8–10: Rep Rnd 1.

Rnd 11: *K2, p2, k2, p1, BUB, p1, k2, p2; rep from * around.

Rnd 12: Rep Rnd 1.

Rep Rnds 1–12 for pat.

Note
Slip all slipped stitches purlwise.

Socks

Leg
Using beading needle, string 80 beads on yarn in sequence A-B-C-D, or as desired, and push down.

Leaving a tail long enough for casting on, make slip knot for long-tail cast-on (see page 17) and put on needle. String 20 more beads on tail.

Cast on 1 st, BUB, *cast on 3 sts, BUB; rep from * 18 times more, end BUB, cast on 1 st—60 sts.

Divide sts evenly on 4 dpns. Join, being careful not to twist sts. Mark as N1 and beg of the rnd.

Socks With a Twinkle
Sample project was knit with Sockotta
(45 per cent cotton/40 per cent
superwash wool/15 per cent
nylon) from Plymouth Yarn Co.

Work in Beaded Rib until all beads have been used. Work 2 more rnds in K2, P2 Rib.

Heel Flap

At beg of next rnd, transfer sts from N3 to N4, turn—30 sts on N4.

Work Heel st as follows:

Row 1 (WS): Sl 1, purl across.

Row 2: *Sl 1, k1; rep from * across.

Rep Rows 1 and 2 for a total of 28 rows, then work Row 1 once more.

Turn Heel

Note: Keep working heel sts as you turn the heel.

Row 1 (RS): *Sl 1, k1; rep from * 9 more times, ssk, turn—8 sts rem unworked.

Row 2: Sl 1, p8, p2tog, turn—8 sts rem unworked.

Row 3: *Sl 1, k1; rep from * 3 more times, sl 1, ssk, turn—7 sts rem unworked.

Row 4: Sl 1, p8, p2tog, turn—7 sts rem unworked.

Continue working in this manner, rep Rows 3 and 4 until all sts have been worked—10 sts rem.

Gusset

Set-up rnd: With RS facing, knit across heel sts using empty dpn as follows: Sl 1, k4; with another needle (N1),

k5, pick up and knit 15 sts along left side of flap; with N2, work 15 instep sts in pat as established; with N3, work rem 15 instep sts in pat as established; with N4, pick up and knit 15 sts along right side of flap, k5 sts from first dpn. Beg of rnd is in centre of heel flap—70 sts divided as follows: N1: 20 sts; N2: 15 sts; N3: 15 sts; N4: 20 sts.

Rnd 1: N1: Knit to last 3 sts, k2tog, k1; N2 and N3: Work across instep st in pat as established; N4: K1, ssk, knit to end of rnd.

Rnd 2: N1: Knit; N2 and N3: Work in pat as established; N4: Knit.

Rep Rnds 1 and 2 until 60 sts rem—15 sts on each needle.

Foot

Work even until foot measures 2 inches less than desired length.

Toe

Rnd 1: N1: *Knit to last 2 sts, k2tog; rep from * on each of the 3 rem needles—56 sts.

Rnd 2: Knit.

Rep [Rnds 1 and 2] 7 times—28 sts.

Rep Rnd 1 until 8 sts rem.

Fasten off, leaving an 8-inch tail.

Using a tapestry needle, pull yarn through the rem sts and pull closed. ∎

BAHAMA MAMA FLIP-FLOP SOCKS

Add some fun to your flip-flops while wearing these whimsical split-toe socks!

Design | Sean Higgins

Sizes

Woman's small (large) to fit shoe sizes 5–7 (8–10) Instructions are given for the smaller size, with larger size in parentheses. When only one number is given, it applies to both sizes.

Finished Measurements

Circumference: 6½ (7¼) inches
Foot length: 9 (9¾) inches

Materials

DK weight yarn (100 yds/50g per ball): 2 (3) balls green
Size 3 (3.25 mm) double-point and 32-inch circular needles or size needed to obtain gauge

Gauge

30 sts and 13 rnds = 4 inches/10 cm in St st.
36 sts and 13 rnds = 4 inches/10 cm in Lace Rib pat.
To save time, take time to check gauge.

Special Abbreviations

Knit in front and back (kf&b): Inc 1 st by knitting in front and back of same st.

N1, N2: Needle 1 (instep sts), Needle 2 (sole sts)

Wrap and Turn (W&T): Bring yarn to RS of work between needles, slip next st purlwise to RH needle, bring yarn around this st to WS, slip st back to LH needle, turn work to begin working back in the other direction.

Work wrapped sts and wraps tog (WW): *On RS:* Knit to wrapped st, slip the wrapped st purlwise from LH needle to RH needle. Use tip of LH needle to pick up wrap(s) and place it/them on RH needle. Slip wrap(s) and st back to LH needle and knit them tog. *On WS:* Purl to wrapped st, slip the wrapped st knitwise from LH needle to RH needle. Use tip of LH to pick up wrap(s) and place it/them on RH needle. Slip wrap(s) and st back to LH needle and purl them tog.

Pattern Stitches

Lace Rib (multiple of 6 sts)

Rnds 1 and 3: *K2, p1; rep from * around.

Rnd 2: *K2, p1, yo, ssk, p1; rep from * around.

Rnd 4: *K2, p1, k2tog, yo, p1; rep from * around.

Rep Rnds 1–4 for pat.

Twisted Rib (multiple of 2 sts)

Rnd 1: *K1-tbl, p1; rep from * around.

Rep Rnd 1 for pat.

Special Techniques

3-Needle Bind-Off: With RS tog and needles parallel, using a 3rd needle, knit tog 1 st from the front needle with 1 from the back. *Knit tog 1 st from the front and back needles, and slip the first st over the 2nd to bind off. Rep from * until required number of sts are bound off.

Picot Bind-Off: *Cast on 3 sts using the cable method (see page 18). Bind off 6 sts. Slip the rem st on the RH needle back to the LH needle. Rep from * around to last st, fasten off last st and weave in end next to beg-of-rnd st to close circle.

Notes

This sock is worked from the toe up (with big toe separated from other 4 toes), has a short-row heel and ends with a Picot Bind-Off.

It begins with a Turkish Cast-On (see page 19) on double-point needles and when there are enough stitches, they are transferred to 1 long needle ("Magic Loop" method see page 22); the pattern can also be easily read for working with 2 circular needles.

The sock is deliberately knit to be snug to allow for stretch of the lace rib pattern.

Elastic yarn knits up at different gauge and yardage based upon tension; use a firm tension on the yarn when knitting.

Socks

Big Toe

Using Turkish Cast-On (see page 19) and 2 dpns, cast on 6 sts (3 sts each needle).

Rnd 1: With 3rd dpn, knit across sts on each needle; mark beg of rnd.

Rnd 2: N1 and N2: [Kf&b] twice, k1—10 sts with 5 on each needle.

Rnd 3 and all odd-numbered rnds: Knit even on both needles.

Rnd 4: N1 and N2: [Kf&b] 4 times, k1—18 sts with 9 on each needle.

Rnd 6: N1 and N2: Kf&b, k6, kf&b, k1—22 sts with 11 on each needle.

Rnd 7: Knit even on both needles.

Size Large Only

Rnd 8: N1 and N2: Kf&b, k8, kf&b, k1—26 sts with 13 on each needle.

Both Sizes

Work even in St st until piece measures 2 inches or reaches the base of your toe; cut yarn.

Sl sts from N1 and N2 to separate pieces of waste yarn and set aside.

4-Toe Section

Work as for Big Toe through Rnd 7 (both sizes)—22 sts with 11 on each needle.

Rnd 8: N1 and N2: [Kf&b, k2] 3 times, kf&b, k1—30 sts with 15 on each needle.

Rnd 9: Knit even on both needles.

Rnd 10: N1: Kf&b, knit to end; N2: knit to last 2 sts, kf&b, k1—32 sts with 16 on each needle.

Rnd 11: Knit all sts.

Rep [Rnds 10 and 11] 6 (7) times—44 (46) sts with 22 (23) on each needle.

Bahama Mama Flip-Flop Socks
Sample project was knit with Fixation Effects (98.3 per cent cotton/1.7 per cent elastic) from Cascade Yarns.

Sl these sts to long circular needle (half the sts on each end of needle [now N1 and N2]) and beg working following Magic Loop method (see page 22).

Work even in St st until piece measures 2 inches or reaches base of toes.

Join Big Toe

Rnd 1: Sl last and first 4 sts of big toe to dpn, leaving rem 14 (18) sts on waste yarn; N1: k18 (19); pull needle/cable of circular needle so that 4 rem sts transfer to N2; N2: using 3-Needle Bind-Off, bind off next 8 sts tog with 8 big toe sts on dpn; k18 (19) sts—50 (56) sts, with 36 (38) sts in 4-toe section and 14 (18) sts in big-toe section.

Rnd 2: N1: K18 (19), pick up and knit 2 sts at join; sl 7 (9) sts from waste yarn onto LH needle and knit them; N2: Sl last 7 (9) sts from waste yarn onto LH needle and knit them; pick up and knit 2 sts at join, k18 (19)—54 (60) sts with 27 (30) sts each needle.

Knit 2 rnds.

Foot

Set-up Lace Rib pat:

Rnd 1: N1: *K2, p1; rep from * to end; N2: knit.

Size Small Only

Rnd 2: N1: *K2, p1, yo, ssk, p1; rep from * to last 3 sts, end k2, p1; N2: knit.

Rnd 3: N1: *K2, p1; rep from * to end; N2: knit.

Rnd 4: N1: *K2, p1, k2tog, p1; rep from * to last 3 sts, end k2, p1; N2: knit.

Size Large Only

Rnd 2: N1: *K2, p1, yo, ssk, p1; rep from * to end; N2: knit.

Rnd 3: N1: *K2, p1; rep from * to end; N2: knit.

Rnd 4: N1: *K2, p1, k2tog, p1; rep from * to end; N2: knit.

Both Sizes

Work even in established Lace Rib (N1) and St st (N2) until foot measures 7½ (8¼) inches from tip of big toe, ending with N1: Rnd 2 or 4.

Heel

Heel is worked back and forth over N2 sts only; instep sts will rem on hold on cable of circular needle.

Row 1: Knit to last st, W&T.

Row 2: Purl to last st, W&T.

Row 3: Knit to first unwrapped st, W&T.

Row 4: Purl to first unwrapped st, W&T.

Rep Rows 3 and 4 until 7 (8) sts are wrapped on each side—13 (14) sts in centre rem unwrapped.

Row 5: Knit to first wrapped st, WW, W&T.

Row 6: Purl to first wrapped st, WW, W&T.

Row 7: Knit to first double-wrapped st, WW, W&T.

Row 8: Purl to first double-wrapped st, WW, W&T.

Rep Rows 7 and 8 until 1 double-wrapped st rem at each end of N2.

Knit to double-wrapped st, WW; do not turn—1 double-wrapped st rem at beg of N2.

Leg

Continue in the round.

N1: Work in established Lace Rib; N2: WW, knit to end.

Beg working established Lace Rib pat all around.

Note: For size small, if desired for ease of working pat, rearrange sts so that there are 30 sts on N1 and 24 on N2.

Work even until leg measures 4½ (5¼) inches from bottom of heel, ending with Rnd 1 or 3.

Work 1½ inches in Twisted Rib.

Using Picot Bind-Off (see page 60), bind off all sts.

Finishing

Weave in ends. Block. ∎

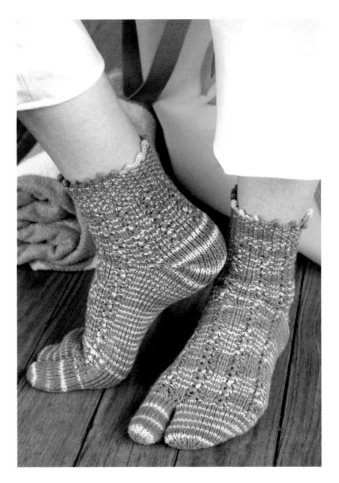

VARIATIONS ON A SOCK

Take a basic sock and add patterns to dress up your feet.

Design | E.J. Slayton

Sizes

Adult's small (medium, large) Instructions are given for smallest size, with larger sizes in parentheses. When only one number is given, it applies to all sizes.

Finished Measurements

Circumference: Approx 7 (8, 9) inches
Foot length: Adjust to fit

Materials

DK weight yarn (174 yds/50 grams per ball):
  2 (2, 3) balls of colour of your choice
Size 4 (3.5mm) set of double-point needles or size
  needed to obtain gauge
Stitch markers
Tapestry needle

Gauge

12 sts and 16 rnds = 2 inches/5cm in St st working in
  rnds.
To save time, take time to check gauge.

Special Abbreviation

N1, N2, N3: Needle 1, Needle 2, Needle 3

Pattern Stitches

Pattern A (multiple of 3 sts)

Rnd 1: Purl.

Rnds 2–4: *K2, p1; rep from * around.

Rep Rnds 1–4 for pat.

Pattern B (multiple of 6 sts)

Rnds 1 and 2: Knit.

Rnd 3: *P1, k5; rep from * around.

Rnd 4: *K1, p1, k3, p1; rep from * around.

Rnd 5: *P1, k1; rep from * around.

Rnd 6: *K1, p1; rep from * around.

Rnd 7: *K2, p1, k1, p1, k1; rep from * around.

Rnd 8: *K3, p1, k2; rep from * around.

Rnds 9 and 10: Knit.

Rnd 11: Rep Rnd 8.

Rnd 12: Rep Rnd 7.

Rnd 13: Rep Rnd 6.

Rnd 14: Rep Rnd 5.

Rnd 15: Rep Rnd 4.

Variations on a Sock

Sample project was knit with Country Style 45 per cent acrylic/40 per cent nylon/15 per cent wool from Sirdar.

Rnd 16: Rep Rnd 3.

Rep Rnds 1–16 for pat.

Pattern C (multiple of 6 sts)

Rnd 1 and all odd-numbered rnds: Knit.

Rnd 2: Knit.

Rnds 4, 6 and 8: *P3, k3; rep from * around.

Rnd 10: Knit.

Rnds 12, 14 and 16: *K3, p3; rep from * around.

Rep Rnds 1–6 for pat.

Pattern D (multiple of 6 sts)

Rnd 1 and all odd-numbered rnds: Knit.

Rnd 2: Purl.

Rnds 4, 6, 8, 10 and 12: *K3, p3; rep from * around.

Rnd 14: Purl.

Rnd 16: Knit.

Rep Rnds 1–16 for pat.

Notes

A variety of pattern stitches are provided. Any of these stitch patterns may be used in the instructions given.

The sample sock shown in photo uses Pattern C.

Socks

Cuff

Cast on 40 (48, 52) sts and join, being careful not to twist.

Work in K2, P2 Rib for 2 inches, inc 2 (0, 2) sts evenly on last rnd—42 (48, 54) sts.

Leg

Purl 1 rnd.

Work in pat of your choice until sock measures 7 inches or desired length to beg of heel.

Arrange sts on needles so there are 21 (25, 27) sts on N1, centring pattern; divide rem 21 (23, 27) instep sts between N2 and N3 to be worked later.

Heel Flap

Working back and forth in rows on N1 sts only, knit 1 row.

Row 1 (WS): Purl.

Row 2: Sl 1, *k1, sl 1; rep from * across.

Rows 3–20 (24, 26): Rep [Rows 1 and 2] 9 (11, 12) times—10 (12, 13) sl st loops on each edge of the heel flap.

Turn Heel

Row 1 (WS): P13 (15, 16), p2tog, p1.

Row 2 (RS): Sl 1, k5, k2tog, k1.

Row 3: Sl 1, p6, p2tog, p1.

Row 4: Sl 1, k7, k2tog, k1.

Row 5: Sl 1, p8, p2tog, p1.

Continue to work in this manner until all sts have been worked, ending with a RS row—13 (15, 17) heel sts rem.

Gusset

With RS facing, using needle with heel sts (N1), pick up and knit 10 (12, 13) sts (1 st in each lp) along edge of heel flap; with N2, knit instep sts from both needles; with N3, pick up and knit 10 (12, 13) sts along other edge of heel flap, k6 (7, 8) sts from N1 to N3—54 (62, 70) sts.

Work St st in rnds from this point.

Rnd 1: Knit.

Rnd 2: N1: Knit to last 3 sts, k2tog, k1; N2: Knit across; N3: K1, ssk, knit to end.

Rnds 3–12(16, 18): Rep [Rnds 1 and 2] 5 (7, 8) times—42 (46, 54) sts.

Foot

Continue to work in St st until foot measures 2 inches less than desired length.

Pattern A

Pattern B

Toe

Arrange sts as follows: N1: 11 (12, 14) sts; N2: 21 (23, 27) sts; N3: 10 (11, 13) sts.

Rnd 1: Knit.

Rnd 2: N1: Knit to last 3 sts, k2tog, k1; N2: K1, ssk, knit to last 3 sts, k2tog, k1; N3: K1, ssk, knit to end.

Rep Rnds 1 and 2 until 18 (18, 22) sts rem. Knit sts from N1 onto N3. Cut yarn, leaving a 15-inch end.

Finishing

Weave toe sts tog using Kitchener Stitch (see page 29). ■

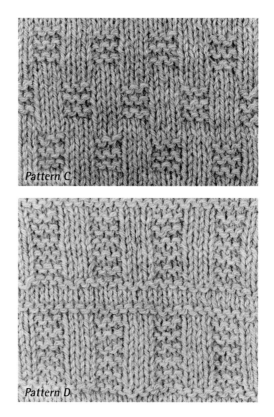

Pattern C

Pattern D

FANCY FAIR ISLE SOCKS

This versatile design, made for either men or women, features self-striping yarns to create impressive results.

Design | Kate Atherley

Sizes

Woman's small (woman's large, man's small, man's large) to fit woman's shoe sizes 5–7 (7½–9, man's shoe size 6–9, 9½–11) Instructions are given for smallest size, with larger sizes in parentheses. When only one number is given, it applies to all sizes.

Finished Measurements

Circumference: 7½ (8, 8½, 9) inches
Foot length: 9 (10, 10, 11) inches

Materials

Sock weight yarn (213 yds/50g per ball):
   2 balls grey (MC)
Sock weight yarn (460 yds/100g per ball):
   1 ball natural/blue/grey multi (CC)
Size 1 (2.25mm) double-point needles (set of 5) or size needed to obtain gauge

Gauge

30 sts and 42 rnds = 4 inches/10cm in both stranded St st and plain St st.
To save time, take time to check gauge.

Special Abbreviation

N1, N2, N3, N4: Needle 1, Needle 2, Needle 3, Needle 4

Notes

This sock is worked on 4 double-point needles from the cuff down, with a heel flap, gusset, and a wedge toe.

Work 2 gauge swatches and if necessary, go up in needle size for stranded stockinette stitch section.

Socks

Cuff & Leg

With MC, cast on 56 (60, 64, 68) sts.

Distribute sts evenly on 4 dpns; place marker for beg of rnd and join, taking care not to twists sts.

Work K1, P1 Rib for 1 inch.

Join CC and work Rnds 1–18 of chart 3 times.

Men's Sizes Only

Work Rnds 1–6 once more.

Cut CC yarn.

Heel Flap

Row 1 (RS): With MC, k14 (15, 16, 17), turn.

Row 2: Sl 1, p27 (29, 31, 33), turn, leaving rem sts on hold on N2 and N3 for instep.

Row 3: Sl 1, knit across heel sts.

Fancy Fair Isle Socks
Sample project was knit with Fortissima Socka (75 per cent wool/25 per cent nylon) from Schoeller Stahl and Step (75 per cent superwash virgin wool/25 per cent nylon) from Austermann.

Row 4: Sl 1, purl across heel sts.

Rep [last 2 rows] 8 (9, 10, 11) times.

Turn Heel
Row 1 (RS): Sl 1, k18 (19, 20, 22), ssk, turn.

Row 2: Sl 1, p10 (10, 10, 12), p2tog, turn.

Row 3: Sl 1, k10 (10, 10, 12), ssk, turn.

Rep last 2 rows until all sts have been worked, ending with a WS row—12 (12, 12, 14) sts.

Gusset
Set-up rnd: With a spare dpn, sl 1, k5 (5, 6); with N1, k6 (6, 6, 7), then pick up and knit 14 (15, 16, 17) sts along left side of flap; with N2 and N3, knit across instep; with N4, pick up and knit 14 (15, 16, 17) sts along right side of flap, then k6 (6, 6, 7) sts from spare dpn. Place marker for beg of rnd in centre of heel—68 (72, 76, 82) sts divided as follows: 20 (21, 22, 24) sts each on N1 and N4; 14 (15, 16, 17) sts each on N2 and N3.

Rnd 1: Knit around, knitting into back loop of all picked-up sts.

Rnd 2 (dec): N1: Knit to last 3 sts, k2tog, k1; N2 and 3: knit across; N4: k1, ssk, knit to end.

Rnd 3: Knit around.

Rep last 2 rnds until 56 (60, 64, 68) sts rem with 14 (15, 16, 17) sts on each needle.

Foot
Work even until foot measures 7 (8, 8, 9) inches or approx 2 inches short of desired length.

Toe
Dec rnd: *N1: Knit to last 3 sts, k2tog, k1; N2: k1, ssk, knit to end; rep from * on N3 and 4—52 (56, 60, 64) sts.

Rep Dec rnd [every 4 rnds] once, [every 3 rnds] twice, [every other rnd] 3 times, then every rnd until 8 sts rem with 2 sts on each needle.

Cut yarn, leaving a 6-inch tail.

Using tapestry needle, thread tail through rem sts, and pull tight and secure on WS.

Finishing
Weave in all ends. Block. ∎

18 17 16 15 14 13 12 11 10 9 8 7 6 5 4 3 2 1	**COLOUR KEY** ■ MC ■ CC

4-st rep

**Fancy Fair
Isle Chart**

WARM THEIR TOES

Keep toes comfy both outside and in the home. You will love these socks for the way they feel inside your boots.

Design | Susan Robicheau

Size
Man's large

Finished Measurement
Circumference: Approx 9¼ inches

Materials
Worsted weight yarn (223 yds/100g per ball):
   2 balls blue
Size 3 (3.25mm) double-point needles (set of 5)
   or size needed to obtain gauge
Stitch marker
Tapestry needle

Gauge
24 sts and 36 rows = 4 inches/10cm in pat st.
To save time, take time to check gauge.

Special Abbreviation
N1, N2, N3, N4: Needle 1, Needle 2, Needle 3, Needle 4

Pattern Stitch
Diagonal Broken Rib (multiple of 8 sts)

Rnd 1: *K1, p1, k1, p5; rep from * around.

Rnd 2 and all even numbered rnds: Knit the knit sts and purl the purl sts.

Rnd 3: *K1, p1, k5, p1; rep from * around.

Rnd 5: *K1, p5, k1, p1; rep from * around.

Rnd 7: *K5, p1, k1, p1; rep from * around.

Rnd 9: *P4, k1, p1, k1, p1; rep from * around.

Rnd 11: *K3, p1, k1, p1, k2; rep from * around.

Rnd 13: *P2, k1, p1, k1, p3; rep from * around.

Rnd 15: *K1, p1, k1, p1, k4; rep from * around.

Rnd 16: Rep Rnd 2.

Note
For smaller-size socks, go down in needle size for tighter gauge; more tightly knit socks will last longer.

Socks

Cuff
Cast on 56 sts. Divide sts evenly on 4 needles (N1: heel, N2 and N3: instep, N4: heel). Place marker for beg of rnd and join without twisting.

Work in k1, p1 rib for 2½ inches.

Leg
Work 4 reps of Diagonal Broken Rib, ending last rnd on N3 (14 sts short of beg of rnd).

Sl sts from N4 to N1 for flap.

Heel Flap

Note: Heel flap is worked on N1 only.

Row 1 (RS): K28.

Row 2 (WS): K1, p12, p2tog, p12, k1—27 sts.

Row 3: K1, *sl 1, k1; rep from * to end.

Row 4: K1, purl to last st, k1.

Rep Rows 3 and 4 until heel flap measures 2¾ inches.

Turn Heel

Row 1 (RS): K14, ssk, k1, turn.

Row 2: Sl 1, p2, p2tog, p1, turn.

Row 3: Sl 1, k3, ssk, k1, turn.

Row 4: Sl 1, p4, p2tog, p1, turn.

Rows 6–14: Continue in this manner, working 1 more st each row before dec—15 sts.

Row 15: Sl 1, k14; do not turn.

Gusset

Rnd 1: With N1, pick up and knit 15 sts along side of heel flap; work in pat as established across N2 and N3; with N4, pick up and knit 15 sts along side of heel flap, then k8 from N1—73 sts.

Rnd 2: N1: Knit to last 3 sts, k2tog, k1; N2 and N3: Work in pat; N4: K1, ssk, knit to end of rnd—71 sts.

Rnd 3: Work even.

Rep [Rnds 2 and 3] 8 times—55 sts.

Foot

Work even until foot measures approx 10 inches from base of heel or approx 2 inches less than desired length, and on last rnd, dec 1 st at beg of N3—54 sts.

Toe

Dec rnd: N1: *Knit to last 3 sts, k2tog, k1; N2: K1, ssk, knit to end; rep from * on N3 and N4—50 sts.

Rep Dec rnd [every other rnd] 7 times—22 sts.

Cut yarn, leaving a 16-inch tail.

Sl sts from N4 to N1 and from N3 to N2—11 sts each needle.

Finishing

Holding N1 and N2 parallel, weave toe sts tog using Kitchener Stitch (see page 29). ■

Warm Their Toes
Sample project was knit with
Classic Merino Wool (100 per cent
wool) from Patons.

MAN'S RACING STRIPE SOCKS

He'll be looking sharp in stripes wearing these socks.

Design | Erssie Major

Sizes
Man's small (large) to fit shoe sizes 6–10 (11–14). Instructions are given for smaller size, with larger size in parentheses. When only one number is given, it applies to both sizes.

Finished Measurements
Circumference: 9 (10) inches
Foot length: 10 (11) inches

Materials
Sock weight yarn (459 yds/100g per ball):
   1 ball blue/grey multi (if making size large with longer leg/foot, an extra ball may be needed)
Size 2 (2.75mm) double-point needles (set of 5) or size to needed to obtain gauge
Size D/3 (3.25mm) crochet hook
Stitch markers, 1 in CC for beg of rnd

Gauge
30 sts and 42 rnds = 4 inches/10cm in St st.
To save time, take time to check gauge.

Special Abbreviations
Wrap and Turn (W&T): Bring yarn to RS of work between needles, slip next st purlwise to RH needle, bring yarn around this st to WS, slip st back to LH needle, turn work to begin working back in the other direction.

Work wrapped sts and wraps tog (WW): *On RS:* Knit to wrapped st, slip the wrapped st purlwise from LH needle to RH needle. Use tip of LH needle to pick up wrap(s) and place it/them on RH needle. Slip wrap(s) and st back to LH needle and knit them tog. *On WS:* Purl to wrapped st, slip the wrapped st knitwise from LH needle to RH needle. Use tip of LH to pick up wrap(s) and place it/them on RH needle. Slip wrap(s) and st back to LH needle and purl them tog.

N1, N2, N3, N4: Needle 1, Needle 2, Needle 3, Needle 4

Make 1 (M1): Insert LH needle from front to back under the running thread between the last st worked and next st on LH needle. With RH needle, knit into the back of this loop.

Pattern Stitch
Wide Rib (multiple of 6 sts)

Rnd 1: *K4, p2; rep from * around.

Rep Rnd 1 for pat.

Special Technique
Provisional Cast-On: With crochet hook and waste yarn, make a chain several sts longer than desired cast on. With knitting needle and project yarn, pick up indicated number of sts in the "bumps" on back of chain. When indicated in pattern, "unzip" the crochet chain to free live sts.

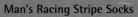

Man's Racing Stripe Socks
Sample project was knit with Step
(75 per cent wool/25 per cent
nylon with jojoba and aloe vera)
from Austermann.

Notes

Socks are worked from the toe-up with short-row toe and heel.

To make both socks match, divide 100g ball evenly into 2 (50g) balls, making sure that each ball begins at the same point in the colour stripe sequence.

Socks

Toe

Divide 100g of sock yarn into 2 equal parts of 50g each.

Using provisional method, cast on 34 (38) sts.

*Row 1 (RS): Knit to last st, W&T.

Row 2: Purl to last st, W&T.

Row 3: Knit to 1 st before previously wrapped st, W&T.

Row 4: Purl to 1 st before previously wrapped st, W&T.

Rep Rows 3 and 4 until 11 (12) sts are wrapped at each side of the toe, leaving 12 (14) sts unwrapped in the centre.

Row 5: Knit to first wrapped st, WW, W&T.

Row 6: Purl to first wrapped st, WW, W&T.

Row 7: Knit to double-wrapped st, WW, W&T.

Row 8: Knit to double-wrapped st, WW, W&T.

Rep Rows 7 and 8 until 2 double-wrapped sts rem (1 at each end).

Row 9: Knit across, WW**, place marker for beg of rnd; unzip Provisional Cast-On and distribute 34 (38) newly live (instep) sts and sole sts as follows: N1 and N2 (instep sts): 16 (19) sts each; N3 and N4 (sole sts): 18 (19) sts each—68 (76) sts.

Foot

Rnd 1: Knit around, working last double-wrapped tog with st when you come to it.

Knit 4 rnds.

Set-up rnd: N1 and N2: [P2, k4] 5 (6) times, p2; N3 and N4: knit.

Work even with Wide Rib on instep sts and St st on sole sts until foot measures approx 9 (10) inches or approx 2 inches short of desired length.

Heel

Size Small Only

Sl 1 st from end of N3 to N2 and 1 st from end of N4 to N1—17 sts on each needle.

Both Sizes

Working on sole sts only, work short-row heel as for toe from * to **.

Leg

Size Small Only

Rnd 1: N1 and N2: Work Wide Rib as established; N3 and N4: continue around in established Wide Rib and dec 1 at beg of N3 and end of N4, working last double-wrapped st when you come to it—66 sts.

Size Large Only

Rnd 1: N1 and N2: Work Wide Rib as established; N3 and N4: continue around in established Wide Rib and M1 at beg of N3 and end of N4, working new sts into pat and working last double-wrapped st when you come to it—78 sts.

Both Sizes

Continue in Wide Rib until sock measures 6 inches or desired length.

Bind off loosely in pat.

Finishing

Weave in all ends. Wash and block to size. ■

SURE-FOOTING SOCKS

This pair will become your favourite every day, everywhere socks.

Design | Fran Ortmeyer

Size
Adult's small (medium, large) Instructions are given for the smallest size, with larger sizes in parentheses. When only one number is given, it applies to all sizes.

Finished Measurements
Circumference: 7½ (8½, 9½) inches
Foot length: Make to desired length

Materials
Sport (worsted, worsted) weight yarn (197 yds/ 85g per ball): 2 balls natural heather (MC), 1 ball cranberry (CC)
Set of double-point needles one size smaller than size needed to obtain gauge for desired size (smaller needles)
Size 8 (5mm) double-point needle *for sizes small and medium*; Size 9 (5.5mm) double-point needles *for size large* or size needed to obtain gauge (larger needles)
Stitch markers

Gauge
20 sts = 3½ inches/9cm on size 8 needles with sport weight yarn.
20 sts = 4 inches/10cm on size 8 needles with worsted weight yarn.
20 sts = 4½ inches/11.5cm on size 9 needles with worsted weight yarn.
To save time, take time to check gauge.

Special Abbreviation
N1, N2, N3: Needle 1, Needle 2, Needle 3

Slip, knit, pass (skp): Slip next st, k1, pass slipped stitch over knit st to dec 1 st.

Notes
Instructions are the same for all sizes. Sock size is determined by gauge achieved on sport or worsted yarn and size needle.

Before beginning, cut 5 yards of main colour from ball and set aside for Heel.

Slip all stitches purlwise with yarn on wrong side of work unless otherwise stated.

Socks

Cuff
With rem MC and smaller needles, loosely cast on 40 sts and distribute as follows: N1: 14 sts; N2: 13 sts; N3: 13 sts. Place marker for beg of rnd and join, being careful not to twist sts.

Rnds 1–6: *K2, p2; rep from * around.

Rnds 7–9: With CC, *k2, p2; rep from * around.

Rnds 10–15: With MC, *k2, p2; rep from * around.

Sure-Footing Socks
Sample project was knit
with Wool-Ease (80 per cent
acrylic/20 per cent wool)
from Lion Brand Yarn Co.

Rnds 16–18: With CC, *k2, p2; rep from * around.

Rnds 19–27: With MC, *k2, p2; rep from * around.

Leg

Knit around until piece measures 11½ inches from cast on, or desired length to bottom of ankle bone.

Drop MC; do not cut.

Change to larger needles

Heel Flap

Row 1: On N1: With CC [sl 1, k1] 10 times, turn, leaving rem 20 sts unworked for instep.

Row 2: Sl 1, p19, turn.

Row 3: [Sl 1, k1] 10 times, turn.

Rows 4–19: Rep [Rows 2 and 3] 8 times.

Row 20: Rep Row 2. Cut CC yarn.

Mark Row 20 for base of heel.

Turn Heel

Row 1: With 5-yd length of MC, sl 1, k12, skp, k1, turn, leaving rem 4 sts unworked—19 sts on needle.

Row 2: Sl 1, p7, p2 tog, p1, turn, leaving rem 4 sts unworked—18 sts.

Row 3: Sl 1, k8, skp, k1, turn, leaving rem 2 sts unworked—17 sts.

Row 4: Sl 1, p9, p2 tog, p1, turn, leaving rem 2 sts unworked—16 sts.

Row 5: Sl 1, k10, skp, k1, turn—15 sts.

Row 6: Sl 1, p11, p2tog, p1, turn—14 sts.

Row 7: Knit next 14 sts; do not turn. Cut off CC.

Gusset

Set-up rnd: With free needle and dropped MC, pick up and knit 10 sts evenly spaced across ends of rows on right side of heel, knit first 7 sts of heel (N1); with separate needle, knit next 7 sts of heel, pick up and knit 10 evenly spaced across ends of rows on left side of heel (N2); with separate needle, knit last 20 unworked MC sts (N3)—54 sts on needles.

Rnd 1: N1: Skp, knit across; N2: Knit to last 2 sts, k2 tog; N3: Knit across—52 sts.

Rnd 2: Knit around.

Rnds 3–12: Rep [Rnds 1 and 2] 5 times.

Rnd 13: Rep Rnd 1—40 sts on needles.

Rnd 14: Redistribute sts as follows: N1: 14 sts; N2: 13 sts; N3: 13 sts.

Foot

Knit until piece measures 2 inches less than desired foot measurement. Cut MC.

Toe

Rnds 1 and 2: With CC, knit around.

Rnd 3: [K2 tog, k14, skp, k1, place marker, k1] twice—36 sts.

Rnd 4: Knit around slipping markers as you come to them.

Rnd 5: [K2tog, knit to 3 sts before next marker, skp, k2] twice—32 sts.

Rnds 6–13: Rep [Rnds 4 and 5] 5 times—16 sts at end of last rnd.

Sl first 7 sts onto first needle; sl next 8 sts onto separate needle, sl last st onto first needle—8 sts on each of two needles.

Cut yarn, leaving 16-inch end for sewing.

Finishing
Using Kitchener Stitch (see page 29), sew stitches on the 2 needles tog. ■

CLASSIC BOOT SOCKS

Take a hike in comfort and style in these traditional-looking socks.

Design | Edie Eckman

Sizes
Adult's medium (large) Instructions are given for smaller size, with larger size in parentheses. When only one number is given, it applies to both sizes.

Finished Measurements
Cuff: 7¾ (8½) inches
Foot length: 8½ (9½) inches

Materials
Worsted weight yarn (200 yds/100g per ball):
   2 skeins grey (MC), 1 skein red (CC)
Size 6 (4mm) double-point needles or size needed to
   obtain gauge
Stitch marker
Tapestry needle

Gauge
24 sts and 32 rnds = 4 inches/10 cm in St st.
To save time, take time to check gauge.

Special Abbreviation
N1, N2, N3: Needle 1, Needle 2, Needle 3

Pattern Stitch
(multiple of 4 sts)

Rnd 1: *K1, p1; rep from * around.

Rnds 2–8: Rep Rnd 1.

Rnd 9: *K1, p3; rep from * around.

Rnds 10–16: Rep Rnd 9.

Rep Rnds 1–16 for pat.

Socks

Cuff
With CC, cast on 40 (48) sts loosely. Divide sts evenly on 3 needles. Join, being careful not to twist sts. Place marker at beg of rnd.

Leg
Work 3 rnds in pat.

Change to MC and knit 1 rnd.

Continue in pat, beg with Rnd 5, and work even for 3 (4) full reps of pat.

Size Medium Only
Rep Rnds 1–8 once.

Heel Flap
Sl last 10 (12) sts of previous rnd to free needle, with same needle, knit first 10 (12) sts of next rnd; sl rem 20 (24) sts to holder for instep.

Break MC, turn and work heel flap in rows with CC.
Purl 1 row.

Classic Boot Socks
Sample project was knit with Berella Muskoka (100 per cent superwash merino wool) from Spinrite Inc.

Leg

Set-up rnd: N1: Work pat as established over first 6 sts, knit to last 6 sts, work pat as established over last 6 sts; N2: work as for N1.

Work even in established pat for 24 (28, 28) rnds [6 (7, 7) reps of rib pat].

Heel Flap

Working back and forth on N1 sts only, work 18 rows in established pat, with sts on N2 on hold for instep.

Turn Heel

Row 1 (RS): K16, ssk, turn.

Row 2: Sl 1, p7, p2tog.

Row 3: Sl 1, k7, ssk.

Rep Rows 2 and 3 until all sts have been worked, ending with Row 2—9 sts rem.

Gusset

Set-up rnd: N1: Knit across 9 heel sts, pick up and knit 9 sts along left side of flap, then pick up and knit 1 st in row below first instep st on N2 (this will prevent a hole); N2: work in established pat across 25 instep sts; N1: pick up and knit 1 st in

row below last instep st on N2, then pick up and knit 9 sts along right side of heel flap, knit across rem sts of N1; N2: work in established pat across; place marker for beg of rnd—54 sts with 29 sts on N1 and 25 sts on N2.

Dec rnd: N1: K1, ssk, knit to last 3 sts, k2tog, k1; N2: work even in established pat—52 sts.

Rnd 2: Work even.

Rep Dec rnd once more—50 sts.

Foot

Work even until foot measures approx 4 (4½, 5) inches from back of heel, ending with Rnd 4 of rib pat.

Toe

Rnd 1 (dec): N1: K5, ssk, knit to last 7 sts, k2tog, k5; N2: work 5 sts in pat, ssk, knit to last 7 sts, k2tog, work 5 sts in pat—46 sts.

Rnd 2: Work even.

Rep [Rnds 1 and 2] 4 times—30 sts.

Rep [Rnd 1] twice more—22 sts with 11 sts on each needle.

Last rnd: N1: K5, k2tog, k4; N2: p1, k4, k2tog, k3, p1—20 sts.

Weave sts from N1 and N2 tog using Kitchener Stitch (see page 29).

Finishing

Weave in ends. Block. ■

**Tickle Your Toes
Top-Down Socks**
Sample project was knit with
Heather (55 per cent merino
superwash wool/30 per cent
cultivated silk/15 per cent nylon)
from The Schaefer Yarn Company.

SIDEWAYS STRIPED SOCKS

Hey, these socks don't match! What a clever way to use those bits of worsted weight yarn.

Design | Lois Young

Sizes
Child's small (medium) Instructions are given for smaller size with larger size in parentheses. If only one number is given, it applies to both sizes.

Finished Measurements
Circumference: 6 (7) inches
Foot length: 7 (8½) inches

Materials
Worsted weight yarn (85 yds/50g per ball):
  1 ball each brown (A), medium blue (B),
  red (C) and dark blue (D)
Size 7 (4.5 mm) double-point needles (set of 4) or size
  needed to obtain gauge (socks)
Stitch markers

Gauge
20 sts and 26 rnds = 4 inches/10cm in St st with
  smaller needles.
To save time, take time to check gauge.

Special Abbreviation
N1, N2, N3: Needle 1, Needle 2, Needle 3

Note
The socks are worked from the cuff down on 3 double-point needles with a heel flap, gussets and wedge toe.

First Sock

Cuff
With dpns and C, loosely cast on 30 (34) sts. Distribute evenly to 3 dpns, place marker for beg of rnd and join, taking care not to twist sts.

Work in K1, P1 Rib until cuff measures 4½ (5) inches or desired length.

Cut C, leaving a 4-inch tail.

Heel Flap
Sl first 14 (16) sts to 1 dpn for heel, and divide rem 16 (18) sts on 2 other dpns to be kept on hold for instep.

Change to B.

Row 1 (RS): Working on heel sts only, sl 1, knit to end.

Row 2: Sl 1, purl to end.

Rep Rows 1 and 2 until 14 (16) rows have been worked.

Turn Heel
Row 1: K7 (8), ssk, k1, turn.

Row 2: Sl 1, p1, p2tog, p1, turn.

Row 3: Sl 1, k3, ssk, k1, turn.

Row 4: Sl 1, p5, p2tog, p1, turn—8 sts.

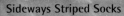

Sideways Striped Socks
Sample project was knit with
1824 Wool (100 per cent merino
superwash wool) from Mission Falls.

Size Medium Only

Row 5: Sl 1, k7, ssk, turn.

Row 6: Sl 1, p7, p2tog, turn—10 sts.

Cut B, leaving a 4-inch tail.

Gusset
Change to A.

Set-up Rnd: N1: Beg at top of heel flap where instep and heel joins, pick up and knit 8 (9) sts along right edge of flap, k4 (5) heel sts; N2: k4 (5) heel sts, pick up and knit 8 (9) sts along left edge of flap; N3: k16 (18) instep sts, place marker for beg of rnd—40 (46) sts distributed as follows: N1: 12 (14) sts; N2: 12 (14) sts; N3: 16 (18) sts.

Rnd 1 (dec): N1: Ssk, knit to end; N2: knit to last 2 sts, k2tog; N3; knit—38 (44) sts.

Rnd 2: Work even.

Rep [Rnds 1 and 2] 5 (6) times—28 (32) sts.

Foot
Work even until foot measures 5½ (6½) inches from back of heel.

Cut A, leaving a 4-inch tail.

Toe
Sl first st on N3 to N2 and last st on N3 to N1—7 (8) sts on N1 and N2 and 14 (16) sts on N3.

Change to D.

Rnd 1 (dec): N1: K1, ssk, knit to end; N2: knit to last 3 sts, k2tog, k1; N3: k1, ssk, knit to last 3 sts, k2tog, k1—24 (28) sts.

Rnd 2: Knit.

Rep Rnds 1 and 2 until 16 sts rem.

Rep Rnd 1 only, until 8 sts rem.

Cut yarn, leaving a 10-inch tail.

Sl sts on N1 to N2.

Finishing
Weave toe sts tog using Kitchener Stitch (see page 29).

Weave in all ends, using tails at beg of heel flap to close and tighten holes that may appear.

Second Sock

Work as for First Sock, but reverse the order of the colours as follows: D, A, B, C. ■

KIDS' BOOT SOCKS

These socks will keep little feet warm inside boots. They also make great house slippers.

Design | E. J. Slayton

Sizes

Child's small (medium, large, extra-large) Instructions are given for smallest size, with larger sizes in parentheses. When only one number is given, it applies to all sizes.

Finished Measurements

Top: 5 (5½, 6, 6½) inches
Foot length: 6½ (7, 7½, 8) inches

Materials

Worsted weight yarn (105 yds/50g per skein):
   1 (2, 3, 3) skeins red (MC), 1 skein blue (CC)
Size 4 (3.5mm) double-pointed needles or size
   needed to obtain gauge
Heel and toe reinforcement thread (optional)
Safety pins
Tapestry needle

4 MEDIUM

Gauge

12 sts and 14 rnds = 2 inches/5cm in St st.
To save time, take time to check gauge.

Special Abbreviation

N1, N2, N3: Needle 1, Needle 2, Needle 3

Notes

Sock top may be worked in Stockinette stitch as shown, or in knit 2, purl 2 ribbing if preferred. When changing colour in ribbing, knit the first round, then resume ribbing pattern.

Socks

Cuff

With MC, cast on 36 (40, 44, 48) sts; join, being careful not to twist.

Work in K2, P2 Rib for 1½ (1½, 2, 2) inches.

Leg

Work 3 rnds MC in St st, 3 rnds CC, then continue in St st until piece measures 5 (5½, 6, 6½) inches or desired length from beg.

Heel Flap

Join CC and knit across 18 (20, 22, 24) sts for heel; divide rem 18 (20, 22, 24) sts between 2 needles for instep to be worked later. MC strand may be left attached.

Working in rows on heel sts only, purl across.

Row 1 (RS): Sl 1, knit to last st, sl 1.

Row 2: Purl.

Rows 3–16 (18, 20, 22): Rep [Rows 1 and 2] 7 (8, 9, 10) times.

Row 17 (19, 21, 23): Rep Rows 1–9, 10, 11, 12 sl st loops on each side of heel flap.

Turn Heel

Place safety pins in sts 6 (7, 8, 9) and 13 (14, 15, 16) to mark centre 8 sts.

Row 1 (WS): P12 (13, 14, 15), p2tog.

Row 2: Sl 1, k6, ssk.

Row 3: Sl 1, p6, p2tog.

Rep Rows 2 and 3 until 8 centre sts rem. Cut CC.

Gusset

With MC, k18 (20, 22, 24) instep sts (N2); with free needle pick up and knit 9 (10, 11, 12) sts in loops along left edge of heel flap, k4 heel sts (N3); knit rem 4 heel sts onto another needle, with same needle, pick up and knit 9 (10, 11, 12) sts in loops along right edge of heel flap (N1). Knit across N2 and N3—44 (48, 52, 56) sts.

Rnd 1: Knit.

Rnd 2: N1: Knit to last 3 sts, k2tog, k1; N2: Knit across; N3: K1, ssk, knit to end.

Rnds 3–8: Rep [Rnds 1 and 2] 3 times—36 (40, 44, 48) sts.

Work even until foot measures 5¼ (5¾, 6¼, 6¾) inches, or approximately 1¼ inches less than desired length.

Toe

Cut MC, attach CC.

Rnd 1: Knit.

Rnd 2: N1: Knit to last 3 sts, k2tog, k1; N2: K1, ssk, knit to last 3 sts, k2tog, k1; N3: K1, ssk, knit to end.

Rep Rnds 1 and 2 until 16 (16, 20, 20) sts rem. With N3, work across sts on N1—8 (8 10, 10) sts each on 2 needles. Cut yarn, leaving an 18-inch end.

Finishing

Weave toe sts tog using Kitchener Stitch (see page 29). ∎

Kids' Boot Socks

Sample project was knit with
Froelich Wolle Aurora (100 per cent
wool) from WheelSmith Wools.

MOSS DIAMONDS & RIB SOCKS

Step out in style with a pair of textured socks in your favourite colour.

Design | E. J. Slayton

Sizes
Adult's small (medium, large) Instructions are given for smallest size, with larger sizes in parentheses. When only one number is given, it applies to all sizes.

Finished Measurements
Cuff: 8½ inches
Foot length: 10 (10½, 11½) inches

Materials
Sock weight yarn (225 yds/50g per skein):
  2 skeins blue
Size 1 (2.5mm) needles or size needed to obtain gauge
Heel and toe reinforcement thread (optional)
Stitch markers
Safety pin
Tapestry needle

1
SUPER FINE

Gauge
16 sts and 20 rnds = 2 inches/5 cm in St st.
To save time, take time to check gauge.

Special Abbreviation
N1, N2, N3: Needle 1, Needle 2, Needle 3

Pattern Stitches
Moss Diamonds (panel of 13 sts)

Note: Chart provided on page 97 for those preferring to work pattern from a chart.

Rnds 1 and 2: K6, p1, k6.

Rnds 3 and 4: K5, p1, k1, p1, k5.

Rnds 5 and 6: K4, p1, [k1, p1] twice, k4.

Rnds 7 and 8: K3, p1, [k1, p1] 3 times, k3.

Rnds 9 and 10: K2, p1, k1, p1, k3, p1, k1, p1, k2.

Rnds 11 and 12: [K1, p1] twice, k5, [p1, k1] twice.

Rnds 13 and 14: K2, p1, k1, p1, k3, p1, k1, p1, k2.

Rnds 15 and 16: K3, p1, [k1, p1] 3 times, k3.

Rnds 17 and 18: K4, p1, [k1, p1] twice, k4.

Rnds 19 and 20: K5, p1, k1, p1, k5.

Rep Rnds 1–20 for pat.

Seed Stitch Rib (multiple of 5 sts)

Rnd 1: *P3, k2; rep from * around.

Rnd 2: *P1, k1, p1, k2; rep from * around.

Rep Rnds 1 and 2 for pat.

Moss Diamonds & Rib Socks

Sample project was knit with Froehlich Wolle Special Blauband (80 per cent wool/20 per cent nylon) from WheelSmith Wools.

Socks

Cuff

Beg at top, cast on 60 (64, 68) sts. Divide sts on 3 needles, mark beg of rnd and join, being careful not to twist. Work in k2, p2 ribbing for 2 inches, inc 1 (2, 3) sts evenly on last rnd—61 (66, 71) sts.

Leg

Set-up pat: Beg with k1 (p2, k2)(k1), work Rnd 1 of Seed St Rib pat across 21 (24, 26) sts, p3, place marker, work Rnd 1 of Diamond pat, place marker, work rem 24 (26, 29) sts in Seed St Rib pat, end p3, k1 (p1)(p3, k1).

Work in established pats until top measures 8½ inches or desired length from beg.

Work first 15 (17, 18) sts of next rnd on N1. Divide next 31 (33, 35) instep sts on N2 and N3, centring diamond pat, sl remaining 15 (16, 18) sts to N1.

Heel Flap

Working on N1 sts only, p30 (33, 36) sts, dec 1 (0, 1) st in centre—29 (33, 35) heel sts.

Row 1: Sl 1, *k1, sl 1; rep from * across.

Row 2: Purl across.

Rep Rows 1 and 2 until there are 15 (16, 17) loops on each side of heel flap, ending with Row 1.

Turn Heel

Place safety pin in st 15 (17, 18). Shaping takes place evenly spaced on each side of this centre st.

Row 1 (WS): P17 (19, 20), p2tog, p1, turn.

Row 2: Sl 1, k6, k2tog, k1, turn.

Row 3: Sl 1, p7, p2tog, p1, turn.

Row 4: Sl 1, k8, k2tog, k1, turn.

Row 5: Sl 1, p9, p2tog, p1, turn.

Row 6: Sl 1, k10, k2tog, k1, turn.

Continue to work in this manner until all sts have been worked, ending with a RS row—17 (19, 21) heel sts.

Gusset

With needle holding heel sts, pick up and knit 15 (16, 17) sts in loops along edge of heel flap (N1); work in established pat across 31 (33, 35) instep sts, working them all onto same needle (N2); with free needle, pick up and knit 15 (16, 17) sts along other edge of heel flap, knit across 8 (9, 10) heel sts (N3)—78 (84, 90) sts.

Rnd 1: Knit to marker, work instep sts in established pat, knit to end.

Rnd 2: Knit to 3 sts from end of N1, k2tog, k1, work in established pat to beg of N 3, k1, ssk, knit to end.

Work [Rnds 1 and 2] 8 (9, 10) times—62 (66, 70) sts.

Foot

Work even as established until foot measures 8 (8½, 9½) inches or approximately 2 inches less than desired length.

Toe

Rnd 1: N1: Knit to last 3 sts, k2tog, k1; N2: K1, ssk, knit to last 3 sts, k2tog, k1; N3: K1, ssk, knit to end.

Rnd 2: Knit.

Rep Rnds 1 and 2 until 26 sts rem, ending with Rnd
1. With N3, knit across sts on N1. Cut yarn, leaving an
18-inch end.

Finishing
Weave toe sts tog using Kitchener Stitch (see page 29). ■

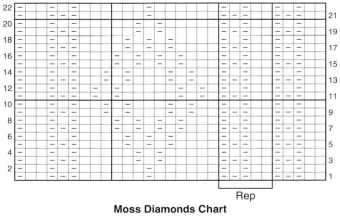

Moss Diamonds Chart

STITCH KEY
☐ K
⊟ P

LEFTOVER SOCKS

Knit these socks using leftover yarn in your teen's favourite colours.

Design | Fran Ortmeyer

Sizes

Adult's small (medium, large) Instructions are given for smallest size, with larger sizes in parentheses. When only one number is given, it applies to all sizes.

Finished Measurements

Circumference: 7½ (8½, 9½) inches
Foot length: Make to desired length.

Materials

Sport (worsted, worsted) weight yarn (solids: 170 yds/100g per ball; prints: 145 yds/85g per ball): 1 ball black (MC), 1 ball each of 5 different colours (CC)
Size 7 (4.5mm) double-point needles *for size small*; Size 7 (4.5mm) double-point needles *for size medium*; Size 8 (5mm) double-point needles *for size large*, or size needed to obtain gauge
2 ring-type stitch markers
Stitch holder

Gauge

23 sts = 3½ inches/9cm in St st on size 7 needles with sport weight yarn.
23 sts = 4 inches/10cm in St st on size 7 needles with worsted weight yarn.
23 sts = 4½ inches/11.5cm in St st on size 8 needles with worsted weight yarn.

Special Abbreviations

N1, N2, N3: Needle 1, Needle 2, Needle 3

Slip, knit, pass (skp): Slip next st, k1, pass slipped stitch over knit st to dec 1 st.

Notes

Instructions are the same for all sizes, sock size is determined by needle size.

Slip all stitches purlwise with yarn on wrong side of work unless otherwise stated.

To change colours, drop last colour to wrong side of work; pick up next colour from under last colour, causing yarns to twist to avoid hole. Carry dropped yarn loosely across wrong side of work; pick up again when needed.

Referring to photo, use contrasting colours randomly; each sock should be different. Cut each colour when no longer needed.

Socks

Cuff

Working loosely, with MC cast 16 sts on each of 3 needles; join being careful not to twist—48 sts.

Rnds 1–9: *K2, p2; rep from * around.

Rnd 10: Working Rnd 10 of Cuff chart (see page 101), k2; using first desired CC, k3, *with MC, k5; with CC, k3; rep from * to last 3 sts, with MC, k3.

Rnds 11–35: Changing colours according to corresponding row of Cuff chart, knit around.

Row 36: With MC, knit around, Drop MC; do not cut.

Heel Flap
Row 1: Working on 1 needle, [sl 1, k1] 12 times—24 sts. Place rem 24 sts on holder for instep.

Row 2: Sl 1, p23, turn.

Row 3: [Sl 1, k1] 12 times, turn.

Rows 4–19: Rep [Rows 2 and 3] 8 times.

Row 20: Rep Row 2.

Mark Row 20 for base of heel.

Turn Heel
Row 1: Sl 1, k12, skp, k1, turn, leaving last 8 sts unworked—23 sts on needle.

Row 2: Sl 1, p3, p2 tog, p1, turn, leaving last 8 sts unworked—22 sts.

Row 3: Sl 1, k4, skp, k1, turn, leaving last 6 sts unworked—21 sts.

Row 4: Sl 1, p5, p2 tog, p1, turn, leaving last 6 sts unworked—20 sts.

Row 5: Sl 1, k6, skp, k1, turn, leaving last 4 sts unworked—19 sts.

Row 6: Sl 1, p7, p2tog, p1, turn, leaving last 4 sts unworked—18 sts.

Leftover Socks
Sample project was knit with Vanna's Choice (100 per cent acrylic) from Lion Brand Yarn Co.

Row 7: Sl 1, k8, skp, k1, turn, leaving last 2 sts unworked—17 sts.

Row 8: Sl 1, p9, p2 tog, p1, turn, leaving last 2 sts unworked—16 sts.

Row 9: Sl 1, k10, skp, p1, turn—15 sts.

Row 10: Sl 1, p11, p2 tog, p1, turn—14 sts.

Row 11: Knit next 14 sts of heel; do not turn. Cut CC yarn.

Gusset

Set-up rnd: With N1 and dropped MC, pick up and knit 10 sts evenly spaced in ends of rows along side of heel flap, knit first 7 sts of heel; with N2, knit next 7 sts of heel, pick up and knit 10 evenly spaced in ends of rows along other side of heel flap; with N3, knit next 24 unworked sts; do not turn—58 sts on needles.

Rnd 1: N1: Skp, knit across; N2, knit to last 2 sts, k2tog; N3; knit across—56 sts

Rnd 2: Knit around.

Rnds 3–12: Rep [Rnds 1 and 2] 5 times—46 sts on needles.

Next rnd: Redistribute sts as follows: N1: K16; N2: k15; N3: k15.

Foot

Measure the length of foot that will wear these socks from base of heel to tip of toe.

Heart (optional for 1 sock)

Knit around until piece measures 1 inch less than half of foot length.

Next rnd: K6, place marker, for Row 1 of Heart chart, k5, with desired CC, k1; with MC, k5, knit around.

Next 9 rnds: Knit to marker; changing colours according to chart, k11; with MC, knit around.

Both socks

Continue in St st until piece measures 2 inches less than desired length of foot.

Toe

Rnd 1: With CC, [k2tog, k17, skp, k1, place marker, k1] twice—42 sts.

Rnd 2: Knit around, slipping markers as you come to them.

Rnd 3: [K2 tog, knit to 3 sts before next marker, skp, k2] twice—38 sts.

Rnds 4–13: Rep [Rnds 2 and 3] 5 times—18 sts at end of last rnd.

Sl first 8 sts onto one needle; sl rem 9 sts onto separate needle, sl last st onto first needle—9 sts on each of 2 needles. Cut yarn, leaving an 18-inch end.

Finishing

Weave toe sts tog using Kitchener Stitch (see page 29). ■

Heart Chart
Each square on chart = 1 knit stitch

STITCH KEY
- ☐ MC
- ⊙ First CC
- ● Second CC
- ☒ Third CC
- ▣ Fourth CC
- ⊡ Fifth CC

Cuff Chart
Each square on chart = 1 knit stitch

SNUGGLY SOCKS

Wear these socks to keep your feet warm while relaxing at home.

Design | Fran Ortmeyer

Sizes
Adult's small (medium, large) Instructions are given for the smallest size, with larger sizes in parentheses. When only one number is given, it applies to all sizes.

Finished Measurements
Circumference: 7½ (8½, 9½) inches
Foot Length: Make to desired length.

Materials
Sport (worsted, worsted) weight yarn (162 yds/ 70g per ball): 1 ball green/brown multi
Size 8 (5mm) double-point needles *for sizes small and medium*; Size 9 (5.5mm) double-point needles *for size large* or size needed to obtain gauge
Stitch markers

Gauge
20 sts = 3½ inches/9cm on size 8 needles with sport weight yarn.
20 sts = 4 inches/10cm on size 8 needles with worsted weight yarn.
20 sts = 4½ inches/11.5cm on size 9 needles with worsted weight yarn.
To save time, take time to check gauge.

Special Abbreviations
N1, N2, N3: Needle 1, Needle 2, Needle 3

Slip, knit, pass (skp): Slip next st, k1, pass slipped stitch over knit st to dec 1 st.

Notes
Instructions are the same for all sizes sock size is determined by gauge achieved on sport or worsted yarn and size needle.

Slip all stitches purlwise with yarn on wrong side of work unless otherwise stated.

Socks

Cuff
Loosely cast on 40 sts and distribute as follows: N1: 14 sts; N2: 13 sts; N3: 13 sts. Place marker for beg of rnd and join, being careful not to twist sts.

Rnds 1–10: *K2, p2; rep from * around.

Leg
Rnds 1–4: Knit around.

Heel Flap
Row 1: On N1: [Sl 1, k1] 10 times, turn, leaving rem 20 sts unworked for instep.

Snuggly Socks
Sample project was knit
with Wool-Ease (80 per cent
acrylic/20 per cent wool)
from Lion Brand Yarn Co.

Row 2: Sl 1, p19, turn.

Row 3: [Sl 1, k1] 10 times, turn.

Rows 4–19: Rep [Rows 2 and 3] 8 times.

Row 20: Rep Row 2. Cut CC yarn.

Mark Row 20 for base of heel.

Turn Heel
Row 1: Sl 1, k12, skp, k1, turn, leaving rem 4 sts unworked—19 sts on needle.

Row 2: Sl 1, p7, p2 tog, p1, turn, leaving rem 4 sts unworked—18 sts.

Row 3: Sl 1, k8, skp, k1, turn, leaving rem 2 sts unworked—17 sts.

Row 4: Sl 1, p9, p2 tog, p1, turn, leaving rem 2 sts unworked—16 sts.

Row 5: Sl 1, k10, skp, k1, turn—15 sts.

Row 6: Sl 1, p11, p2tog, p1, turn—14 sts.

Row 7: K14 sts; do not turn. Cut yarn.

Gusset
Set-up rnd: With free needle, pick up and knit 10 sts evenly spaced across ends of rows on right side of heel, knit first 7 sts of heel (N1); with separate needle, knit next 7 sts of heel, pick up and knit 10 evenly spaced across ends of rows on left side of heel (N2); with separate needle, knit last 20 unworked MC sts (N3)—54 sts on needles.

Rnd 1: N1: Skp, knit across; N2: Knit to last 2 sts, k2 tog; N3: Knit across—52 sts.

Rnd 2: Knit around.

Rnds 3–14: Rep [Rnds 1 and 2] 6 times—40 sts on needles.

Rnd 15: Redistribute sts as follows: N1: 14 sts; N2: 13 sts; N3: 13 sts.

Foot
Measure the length of foot that will wear these socks from base of heel to tip of toe.

Knit until piece measures 2 inches less than desired foot measurement.

Toe
Rnd 1: [K2 tog, k14, skp, k1, place marker, k1] twice—36 sts.

Rnd 2: Knit around slipping markers as you come to them.

Rnd 3: [K2tog, knit to 3 sts before next marker, skp, k2] twice—32 sts

Rnds 4–11: Rep [Rnds 2 and 3] 4 times—16 sts at end of last rnd.

Sl first 7 sts onto first needle; sl next 8 sts onto separate needle, sl last st onto first needle—8 sts on each of two needles.

Cut yarn, leaving 16-inch end for sewing.

Finishing
Weave toe sts on two needles tog using Kitchener Stitch (see page 29). ■

BABY CABLES BOOTIE SOCKS

Knit up these cute socks with simple cables. They can be worn any season of the year.

Design | Dawn Brocco

Sizes

Infant's size 3 (6, 12) months Instructions are given for smallest size, with larger sizes in parentheses. When only one number is given, it applies to all sizes.

Finished Measurements

Circumference: 4 (4 ½, 5) inches
Foot length: 3¾ (4¼, 4¾) inches
Heel to top of cuff: 3¾ (3¾, 4½) inches

Materials

DK weight yarn (115 yds/50g per skein):
    1 skein blue
Size 2 (2.75mm) double-pointed needles or size needed
    to obtain gauge
Tapestry needle

Gauge

7 sts and 10 rows = 1 inch/2.5 cm in St st.
To save time, take time to check gauge.

Special Abbreviation

N1, N2, N3: Needle 1, Needle 2, Needle 3

Pattern Stitch

Baby Cable Rib

Rnds 1, 2 and 4: *K2, p2; rep from * around.

Rnd 3: *K1 in 2nd st on LH needle, k1 in first st, sl both sts off tog, p2, rep from * around.

Rep Rnds 1–4 for pat.

Socks

Leg

Cast on 32 (36, 40) sts, divide on 3 needles. Mark beg of rnd and work in Baby Cable Rib pat for 16 (16, 20) rnds.

Heel Flap

K16 (18, 20) sts. Work in St st on these 16 (18, 20) sts for 15 (17, 19) more rows, ending on a WS row.

Shape Heel

Row 1: K8 (9, 10) sts, ssk, k1, turn.

Row 2: Sl 1, p1, p2tog, p1, turn.

Row 3: Sl 1, k2, ssk, k1, turn.

Row 4: Sl 1, p3, p2tog, p1, turn.

Row 5: Sl 1, k4, ssk, k1, turn.

Row 6: Sl 1, p5, p2tog, p1, turn.

Size 3 Months Only

Row 7: Sl 1, k6, ssk, turn.

Row 8: Sl 1, p6, p2tog, turn—8 sts rem.

Size 6 Months Only
Row 7: Sl 1, k6, ssk, k1, turn.

Row 8: Sl 1, p7, p2tog, p1, turn—10 sts rem.

Size 12 Months Only
Row 7: Sl 1, k6, ssk, k1, turn.

Row 8: Sl 1, p7, p2tog, p1, turn.

Row 9: Sl 1, k8, ssk, turn.

Row 10: Sl 1, p8, p2tog, turn—10 sts rem.

Turn Heel
Sl 1, k7 (9, 9), with same needle, pick up and knit 8 (9, 10) sts along right edge of heel flap (N1); with separate needle and, beg with Rnd 1, work in established Baby Cable Rib pat across next 16 (18, 20) sts (N2); with separate needle, pick up and knit 8 (9, 10) sts along left edge of heel flap, with same needle, k4 (5, 5) heel sts (N3). Rnds now begin at centre heel.

Gusset
Rnd 1: Knit.

Rnd 2: N1: Knit to last 3 sts, ssk, k1; N2: Work in Baby Cable Rib pat across; N3: K1, k2tog, knit to end.

Rep Rnds 1 and 2 until 32 (36, 40) sts rem.

Foot
Work even in established pats (St st for bottom and cable rib for top), until 20 (24, 28) rnds of Baby Cable Rib pat are completed, counting from beg of instep.

Toe
Sizes 3 Months and 12 Months Only
Rnd 1: *K6, k2tog; rep from * around.

Rnds 2, 4, 6, 8 and 10: Knit.

Rnd 3: *K5, k2tog; rep from * around.

Rnd 5: *K4, k2tog; rep from * around.

Rnd 7: *K3, k2tog; rep from * around.

Rnd 9: *K2, k2tog; rep from * around.

Rnd 11: *K1, k2tog; rep from * around.

Rnd 12: [K2tog] around—4 (5) sts rem.

Size 6 Months Only
Work Rnds 5–12 of Toe as above—6 sts rem.

Finishing
Cut yarn. With tapestry needle, pull through rem sts and fasten off. ∎

Baby Cable Bootie Socks

Sample project was knit with Magic
Garden Cotton Candy (70 per cent
cotton/30 per cent wool) from Naturally.

LITTLE TIKE TOE-UP SOCKS

Kiddies' feet will stay warm in these eye-catching socks.

Design | Nazanin S. Fard

Sizes

Child's small (medium) Instructions are given for smaller size, with larger size in parentheses. When only one number is given, it applies to both sizes.

Finished Measurements

Circumference: 5 (6½) inches
Foot length: 5 (7) inches

Materials

Sock weight yarn (462 yds/100g per ball):
  1 ball self-striping brights
2 size 3 (3.25mm) 24-inch circular needles or size needed to obtain gauge
Size F/5 (3.75mm) crochet hook

Gauge

28 sts and 36 rnds = 4 inches/10cm in St st.
To save time, take time to check gauge.

Special Abbreviations

N1, N2: Needle 1 (sole), Needle 2 (instep)

Wrap and Turn (W&T): Bring yarn to RS of work between needles, slip next st purlwise to RH needle, bring yarn around this st to WS, slip st back to LH needle, turn work to begin working back in the other direction.

Work wrapped sts and wraps tog (WW): *On RS:* Knit to wrapped st, slip the wrapped st purlwise from LH needle to RH needle. Use tip of LH needle to pick up wrap(s) and place it/them on RH needle. Slip wrap(s) and st back to LH needle and knit them tog. *On WS:* Purl to wrapped st, slip the wrapped st knitwise from LH needle to RH needle. Use tip of LH to pick up wrap(s) and place it/them on RH needle. Slip wrap(s) and st back to LH needle and purl them tog.

Make 1 Left (M1L): Insert LH needle from front to back under the running thread between the last st worked and next st on LH needle. With RH needle, knit into the back of this loop.

Make 1 Right (M1R): Insert LH needle from back to front under the running thread between the last st worked and next st on LH needle. With RH needle, knit into the front of this loop.

Pattern Stitch

Eyelet Rib (multiple of 5 sts + 2)

Rnd 1: P2, *k3, p2; rep from * to end.

Rnd 2: P2, *k1, yo, k2tog, p2; rep from * to end.

Rnds 3 and 4: Rep Rnd 1.

Rep Rnds 1–4 for pat.

Note: When working all-around for leg, work established 5-st rep only.

Little Tike Toe-Up Socks
Sample project was knit with
Trekking XXL (75 per cent wool/
25 per cent nylon) from Zitron.

Special Technique

Provisional Cast-On: With crochet hook and waste yarn, make a chain several sts longer than desired cast on. With knitting needle and project yarn, pick up indicated number of sts in the "bumps" on back of chain. When indicated in pattern, "unzip" the crochet chain to free live sts.

Notes

This sock is worked on 2 circular needles from the toe up, with a short-row toe, a gusset and a short-row heel.

One ball of yarn will make 3 pairs of small-sized socks or 2 pairs of medium-sized socks.

Socks

Toe

Using Provisional Cast-On method and 1 circular needle (N1), cast on 18 (23) sts.

Row 1 (WS): Purl.

Row 2: Knit to last st, W&T.

Row 3: Purl to last st, W&T.

Row 4: Knit to st before last wrapped st, W&T.

Row 5: Purl to st before last wrapped st, W&T.

Rep Rows 4 and 5 until 6 (11) sts rem unwrapped.

Row 6: Knit to the first wrapped st, WW, W&T.

Row 7: Purl to the first wrapped st, WW, W&T.

Row 8: Knit to the first double-wrapped st, WW, W&T.

Row 9: Purl to the first double-wrapped st, WW, W&T.

Rep Rows 8 and 9 until 1 double-wrapped st rem at each end of work.

Foot

Rnd 1: Knit to double-wrapped st, WW, do not turn; unzip Provisional Cast-On and sl 17 (22) newly live sts to 2nd circular needle (N2) for instep and work Eyelet Rib across new sts, place marker for beg of rnd—35 (45) sts.

Rnd 2: N1: WW, knit to end; N2: work Eyelet Rib across.

Continue in St st (sole) and Eyelet Rib (instep) until 4 (7) total pat reps are complete.

Gusset

Rnd 1: N1: K1, M1R, knit to last st, M1L, K1; N2: work in established pat—37 (47) sts.

Rnd 2: N1: Knit; N2: work in established pat.

Rep Rnds 1 and 2 until there are 30 (41) sts on N1.

Heel

Row 1 (RS): On N1, k23 (31), W&T.

Row 2: P16, W&T.

Row 3: Knit to st before last wrapped st, W&T.

Row 4: Purl to st before last wrapped st, W&T.

Rep Rows 3 and 4 until 10 (13) sts rem unwrapped in centre.

Row 5 (RS): Knit to the first wrapped st, WW, W&T.

Row 6: Purl to the first wrapped st, WW, W&T.

Row 7: Knit to the first double-wrapped st, WW, W&T.

Row 8: Purl to the first double-wrapped st, WW, W&T.

Rep Rows 8 and 9 until all double-wrapped sts are worked.

Turn Heel

Row 1: Sl 1, knit to 1 st before gap, ssk, turn.

Row 2: Sl 1, purl to 1 st before gap, p2tog, turn.

Rep Rows 1 and 2 until 1 st rem outside gap at each end.

Leg

Rnd 1: N1: Sl 1, knit to 1 st before gap, ssk; N2: work in established Eyelet Rib.

Rnd 2: N1: K2tog, knit to end; N2: work in Eyelet Rib—35 (45) sts with 18 (23) sts on N1 and 17 (22) sts on N2.

Rnd 3: N1: Continue 5-st rep of Eyelet Rib as already established on N2; N2: work in Eyelet Rib.

Work even in Eyelet Rib all around until leg measures 2 inches, ending on Rnd 4.

Cuff

Rnd 1: K2tog, *p1, k1; rep from * around—34 (44) sts.

Rnds 2–10: *K1, p1; rep from * around.

Bind off all sts loosely in rib.

Finishing

Weave in loose ends. Block as desired. ∎

WEE BABY BAMBOOZLE SOCKS

These multicoloured socks will be bright and cheery for Baby to wear.

Design | Laura Andersson

Sizes

Newborn (3–6, 6–9, 9–12, 12–18) months

Instructions are given for smallest size, with larger size(s) in parentheses. When only one number is given, it applies to all sizes.

Finished Measurements

Circumference: 3¾ (3¾, 4¼, 5, 5¾) inches
Foot length: 3½ (3½, 4, 4, 4½) inches

Materials

Worsted weight yarn (90 yds/50g per ball):
   1 ball each yellow (MC), green multi (A),
   green (B), and limeade (C)
Size 4 (3.5mm) double-point needles or size needed to
   obtain gauge
Stitch markers, 1 in CC for beg of rnd

Gauge

22 sts and 36 rnds = 4 inches/10cm in St st and stranded
   St st.
To save time, take time to check gauge.

Special Abbreviation

N1, N2, N3: Needle 1, Needle 2, Needle 3

Notes

The sock is worked on 3 double-point needles from the cuff down, with a heel flap, gusset and wedge toe.

Work 2 gauge swatches and if necessary, go up in needle size for stranded stockinette section.

Socks

Cuff

With MC and dpn, cast on 20 (20, 24, 28, 32) sts.
Do not join.

Purl 1 row, distributing sts on 3 dpn; place marker for beg of rnd and join, taking care not to twist sts.

Rnds 1–4: With MC, work in K2, P2 Rib. Cut MC.

Rnds 5–9: Change to A and continue in established rib.

Rnd 10: Purl around. Cut A.

Rnds 11–15: Change to B; [knit 1 rnd, purl 1 rnd] twice, knit 1 rnd.

Rnds 16 and 17: Join C; *k2 B, k2 C; rep from * around.

Rnds 18 and 19: *K2 C, k2 B; rep from * around. Cut B.

Rnds 20 and 21: With C, purl around.

Rnds 22 and 23: Join A; *k2 A, k2C; rep from * around.

Rnds 24 and 25: *K2 C, k2 A; rep from * around. Cut C.

Rnds 26 and 27: Join MC; *k2 A, k2 MC; rep from * around.

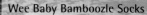

Wee Baby Bamboozle Socks
Sample project was knit with
Bamboozle (55 per cent bamboo/
24 per cent cotton/21 per cent elastic
nylon) from Crystal Palace Yarns.

Rnds 28 and 29: *K2 MC, k2 A; rep from * around.

Rnd 30: With A, purl around.

Rnd 31: With MC, purl around.

Rnds 32–34: With A, knit around.

Rnds 35–37: With MC, knit around. Cut MC.

Heel Flap

Row 1 (RS): Change to A; k6 (6, 7, 7, 8) sts, turn.

Row 2: P12 (12, 14, 14, 16) for heel; sl rem 8 (8, 10, 14, 16) sts to 1 or 2 dpn for instep.

Row 3: *Sl 1, k1; rep from * across.

Row 4: Sl 1, purl to end of row.

Rep Rows 3 and 4 until the heel flap measures 1 (1, 1¼, 1¼, 1½) inches.

Turn Heel

Row 1 (RS): Sl 1, k6 (6, 7, 7, 8), ssk, k1, turn.

Row 2: Sl 1, p3, p2tog, p1, turn.

Row 3: Sl 1, knit to 1 st before gap, ssk, k1, turn.

Row 4: Sl 1, purl to 1 st before gap, p2tog, p1, turn.

Rep Rows 3 and 4 until all sts are used. If necessary, omit the k1 and p1 following dec on last 2 rows— 8 (8, 8, 8, 10) sts.

Gusset

Set-up rnd: With a spare dpn, k4 (4, 4, 4, 5); with N1, k4 (4, 4, 4, 5), then pick up and knit 1 st in each of the slipped sts along the side of flap; with N2, work instep sts in rib as follows: p1 (1, 2, 2, 1), k2, *p2, k2; rep from * to last 1 (1, 2, 2, 1) instep st(s), p1 (1, 2, 2, 1); with N3, pick up and knit 1 st in each of the slipped sts along the side of flap, then knit sts from the spare dpn. Place marker for beg of rnd in centre of heel.

Rnd 1: Work even in pat as established. Cut A.

Rnd 2 (dec): Change to B and work as follows: N1: knit to last 3 sts, k2tog, k1; N2: work established rib; N3: k1, ssk, knit to end of rnd.

Work last 2 rnds until 20 (20, 24, 28, 32) sls rem.

Foot
Work even until foot measures 3 (3, 3½, 3½, 3½) inches. Cut B.

Toe
Rnd 1 (dec): Change to MC; N1: knit to last 3 sts, k2tog, k1; N2: k1, ssk, knit to last 3 sts, k2tog, k1—16 (16, 20, 24, 28) sts.

Rnd 2: Knit around.

Rep [Rnds 1 and 2] 0 (0, 0, 1, 2) time(s)—16 (16, 20, 20, 20) sts.

Rep [Rnd 1] 2 (2, 3, 3, 3) times—8 sts.

Cut yarn, leaving an 8-inch tail.

Using tapestry needle, thread tail through rem sts, and pull tight. Secure on WS.

Finishing
Weave in all ends. Block. ■

KIRSTEN SOCKIES

These delightful baby socks feature accent picot edging and contrasting yarns, creating eye-catching results.

Design | Patti Pierce Stone

Sizes

Infant/Child (3–6, 6–9, 9–12, 12–18) months to fit shoe sizes 1 (3, 4, 5, 8) Instructions are given for smallest size, with larger sizes in parentheses. When only one number is given, it applies to all sizes.

Materials

DK weight yarn (108 yds/50g per skein):
   1 (1, 1, 2, 2) skeins lavender (MC) and 1 skein white (CC)

Size 3 (3.25mm) 24-inch circular needle and spare needle (of any sort) or size needed to obtain gauge
Size 4 (3.5mm) 29-inch (or longer) circular needle and spare needle (of any sort)
Size E/4 (3.5mm) crochet hook
Stitch markers, 1 in CC for beg of rnd

Gauge

23 sts and 29 rnds = 4 inches/10cm in St st on smaller needle.
To save time, take time to check gauge.

Special Technique

Provisional Cast-On: With crochet hook and waste yarn, make a chain several sts longer than desired cast on. With knitting needle and project yarn, pick up indicated number of sts in the "bumps" on back of chain. When indicated in pattern, "unzip" the crochet chain to free live sts.

Notes

The pattern for the sockies is written so that the project is knit on one circular needle using the "Magic Loop" method (see page 22). You can opt to work on double-pointed or 2 circular needles.

The socks are worked from the top down with a picot hem, semi-wrapped short-row heel and wedge toe.

When working the semi-wrapped short-row heel, slip first stitch of each row purlwise with yarn in back.

Socks

Picot Border

Using provisional method, smaller needle and MC, cast on 24 (26, 28, 32, 34) sts, distribute sts evenly as for Magic Loop (heel sts on first needle tip, instep sts on 2nd needle tip); place marker for beg of rnd and join, being careful not to twist sts.

Knit 4 rnds.

Turning rnd: K1, *yo, k2tog; rep from * to last st, end yo, knit last st on rnd tog with first st on next rnd.

Knit 4 rnds.

Join hem: **Unzip waste yarn from approx 25 per cent of Provisional Cast-On sts; sl live sts to spare needle the same size as main needle; holding the 2 needles parallel with RS of fabric facing and using larger needle and CC, *knit

Kirsten Sockies
Sample project was knit with Cotton Classic (100 per cent mercerized cotton) from Tahki•Stacy Charles.

PIXIE BOOTIES

Spread a little "pixie dust" with these enchanting booties.

Design | Erssie Major

Sizes

Infant's 0–3 (3–6, 6–9, 9–12, 12–18) months Instructions are given for smallest size, with larger sizes in parentheses. When only one number is given, it applies to all sizes.

Finished Measurements

Circumference: 4¼ (5, 5¾, 6½, 7¼) inches
Foot length: 3½ (3¾, 4, 4¼, 4¾) inches

Materials

DK weight yarn (131 yds/50g per hank):
  1 (1, 2, 2, 2) hanks in multi-colours
Size 6 (4mm) double-point needles (set of 5) or size
  needed to obtain gauge.
Stitch marker

Gauge

22 sts and 28 rnds = 4 inches/10cm in St st.
To save time, take time to check gauge.

Special Abbreviations

N1, N2, N3, N4: Needle 1, Needle 2, Needle 3, Needle 4

Wrap and Turn (W&T): Bring yarn to RS of work between needles, slip next st purlwise to RH needle, bring yarn around this st to WS, slip st back to LH needle, turn work to begin working back in the other direction.

Work wrapped sts and wraps tog (WW): *On RS:* Knit to wrapped st, slip the wrapped st purlwise from LH needle to RH needle. Use tip of LH needle to pick up wrap(s) and place it/them on RH needle. Slip wrap(s) and st back to LH needle and knit them tog. *On WS:* Purl to wrapped st, slip the wrapped st knitwise from LH needle to RH needle. Use tip of LH to pick up wrap(s) and place it/them on RH needle. Slip wrap(s) and st back to LH needle and purl them tog.

Notes

The socks are worked from the cuff down on 4 double-point needles with a picot hem, short-row heel and wedge toe.

Needle 1 and Needle 2 hold heel/sole stitches; Needle 3 and Needle 4 hold instep stitches.

Booties

Cuff

Cast on 24 (28, 32, 36, 40) sts and distribute evenly on 4 dpns with 6 (7, 8, 9, 10) sts on each dpn; place marker for beg of rnd and join, taking care not to twist sts.

Knit 6 rnds.

Next rnd (picot turning edge): *Yo, k2tog; rep from * around.

Knit 6 rnds.

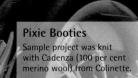

Pixie Booties
Sample project was knit with Cadenza (100 per cent merino wool) from Colinette.

Next rnd (joining rnd): With LH needle, pick up first cast-on st, then knit it tog with first st of rnd, *pick up next cast-on st and knit it tog with next st; rep from * around, joining hem. Knit 8 (10, 10, 12, 12) rnds.

Purl 1 rnd (turning rnd).

Turn work and start working rnd in opposite direction so that WS becomes RS and cuff folds back on purl edge.

Leg
Knit 15 (17, 17, 19, 19) rnds.

Next rnd: *K2, yo, k2tog; rep from * around.

Knit 5 rnds.

Heel
Sl sts on N2 to N1 for heel, leaving rem sts on hold on N3 and N4 for instep.

Row 1 (RS): Working on heel sts only, knit to last st, W&T.

Row 2: Purl to last st, W&T.

Row 3: Knit to 1 st before previously wrapped st, W&T.

Row 4: Purl 1 st before previously wrapped st, W&T.

Rep Rows 3 and 4 until 4 (4, 5, 6, 6) sts are wrapped on each side of the toe, leaving 4 (6, 6, 6, 8) sts unwrapped in the centre.

Row 5: Knit to first wrapped st, WW, W&T.

Row 6: Purl to first wrapped st, WW, W&T.

Row 7: Knit to first double-wrapped st, WW, W&T.

Row 8: Purl to first double-wrapped st, WW, W&T.

Rep Rows 7 and 8 until all sts have been worked and 1 double-wrapped st rem at each end.

Foot
Rnd 1: With N1, k6 (7, 8, 9, 10); with N2, knit to double-wrapped st, WW; with N3 and N4: knit across, place marker for beg of rnd.

Rnd 2: WW last double-wrapped st, knit around.

Work even in St st until foot measures approx 2¾ (3, 3¼, 3½, 4) inches or ¾ inch short of desired length.

Toe

Dec rnd: N1: K1, ssk, knit to end; N2: knit to last 3 sts, k2tog, k1; N3 and N4: work as for N1 and N2—20 (24, 26, 32, 36) sts.

Rep Dec rnd until 8 sts rem.

Weave toe sts tog using Kitchener Stitch (see page 29).

Twisted Cords

Cut 3 strands each 1 yd long. Fold in half, tie ends tog, and secure folded end to a stationary object. Twist yarn until it begins to double back on itself. Fold in half again with both ends together and allow to twist upon itself. Tie a knot a short distance from each end, then cut end to make a small tassel. Tie 2 more knots on either side of the centre of the cord, then cut between these 2 knots, resulting in 2 twisted cords.

Thread each cord through eyelets on each of the booties and tie bows at front.

Weave in all ends. ■

INDEX

INDEX

Metric Conversion Charts

METRIC CONVERSIONS				
yards	x	.9144	=	metres (m)
yards	x	91.44	=	centimetres (cm)
inches	x	2.54	=	centimetres (cm)
inches	x	25.40	=	millimetres (mm)
inches	x	.0254	=	metres (m)

| centimetres | x | .3937 | = | inches |
| metres | x | 1.0936 | = | yards |

INCHES INTO MILLIMETRES & CENTIMETRES (Rounded off slightly)

inches	mm	cm	inches	cm	inches	cm	inches	cm
1/8	3	0.3	5	12.5	21	53.5	38	96.5
1/4	6	0.6	5½	14	22	56	39	99
3/8	10	1	6	15	23	58.5	40	101.5
1/2	13	1.3	7	18	24	61	41	104
5/8	15	1.5	8	20.5	25	63.5	42	106.5
3/4	20	2	9	23	26	66	43	109
7/8	22	2.2	10	25.5	27	68.5	44	112
1	25	2.5	11	28	28	71	45	114.5
1¼	32	3.2	12	30.5	29	73.5	46	117
1½	38	3.8	13	33	30	76	47	119.5
1¾	45	4.5	14	35.5	31	79	48	122
2	50	5	15	38	32	81.5	49	124.5
2½	65	6.5	16	40.5	33	84	50	127
3	75	7.5	17	43	34	86.5		
3½	90	9	18	46	35	89		
4	100	10	19	48.5	36	91.5		
4½	115	11.5	20	51	37	94		

KNITTING NEEDLES CONVERSION CHART

Canada/U.S.	0	1	2	3	4	5	6	7	8	9	10	10½	11	13	15
Metric (mm)	2	2¼	2¾	3¼	3½	3¾	4	4½	5	5½	6	6½	8	9	10

CROCHET HOOKS CONVERSION CHART

Canada/U.S.	1/B	2/C	3/D	4/E	5/F	6/G	8/H	9/I	10/J	10½/K	N
Metric (mm)	2.25	2.75	3.25	3.5	3.75	4.25	5	5.5	6	6.5	9.0

Skill Levels

BEGINNER

Projects for first-time knitters using basic knit and purl stitches. Minimal shaping.

EASY

Projects using basic stitches, repetitive stitch patterns, simple colour changes and simple shaping and finishing.

INTERMEDIATE

Projects with a variety of stitches, such as basic cables and lace, simple intarsia, double-pointed needles and knitting-in-the-round needle techniques, mid-level shaping and finishing.

EXPERIENCED

Projects using advanced techniques and stitches, such as short rows, Fair Isle, more intricate intarsia, cables, lace patterns and numerous colour changes.

FEELING CRAFTY? GET CREATIVE!

Each 160-page book features easy-to-follow, step-by-step instructions and full-page colour photographs of every project. Whatever your crafting fancy, there's a Company's Coming Creative Series craft book to match!

Beading: Beautiful Accessories in Under an Hour
Complement your wardrobe, give your home extra flair or add an extra-special personal touch to gifts with these quick and easy beading projects. Create any one of these special crafts in an hour or less.

Knitting: Easy Fun for Everyone
Take a couple of needles and some yarn and see what beautiful things you can make! Learn how to make fashionable sweaters, comfy knitted blankets, scarves, bags and other knitted crafts with these easy-to-intermediate knitting patterns.

Card Making: Handmade Greetings for All Occasions
Making your own cards is a fun, creative and inexpensive way of letting someone know you care. Stamp, emboss, quill or layer designs in a creative and unique card with your own personal message for friends or family.

Patchwork Quilting
In this book full of throws, baby quilts, table toppers, wall hangings—and more—you'll find plenty of beautiful projects to try. With the modern fabrics available, and the many practical and decorative applications, patchwork quilting is not just for Grandma!

Crocheting: Easy Blankets, Throws & Wraps
Find projects perfect for decorating your home, for looking great while staying warm or for giving that one-of-a-kind gift. A range of simple but stunning designs make crocheting quick, easy and entertaining.

Sewing: Fun Weekend Projects
Find a wide assortment of easy and attractive projects to help you create practical storage solutions, decorations for any room or just the right gift for that someone special. Create table runners, placemats, baby quilts, pillows and more!

For a complete listing of Company's Coming cookbooks and craft books, check out

www.companyscoming.com

We have a tasty lineup of cookbooks, with plenty more in the oven.

www.companyscoming.com

- Preview new titles
- Exclusive cookbook offers
- Find titles no longer in stores

Sign up for our FREE newsletter and receive kitchen-tested recipes twice a month!